How to access the supplemental web resource

We are pleased to provide access to a web resource that supplements you textbook, *Complete Guide to Primary Dance.* This resource offers a bank photos, video clips, warm-ups and written resources to assist you in your teaching.

Accessing the web resource is easy! Follow these steps if you purchased a new book:

1. Visit www.HumanKinetics.com/CompleteGuidetoPrimaryDance.

2. Click the <u>first edition</u> link next to the book cover.

3. Click the Sign In link on the left or top of the page. If you do not have an account with Human Kinetics, you will be prompted to create one.

4. If the online product you purchased does not appear in the Ancillary Items box on the left of the page, click the Enter Key Code option in that box. Enter the key code that is printed at the right, including all hyphens. Click the Submit button to unlock your online product.

5. After you have entered your key code the first time, you will never have to enter it again to access this product. Once unlocked, a link to your product will permanently appear in the menu on the left. For future visits, all you need to do is sign in to the textbook's website and follow the link that appears in the left menu!

→ Click the Need Help? button on the textbook's website if you need assistance along the way.

How to access the web resource if you purchased a used book:

You may purchase access to the web resource by visiting the text's website, **www.HumanKinetics.com/CompleteGuidetoPrimaryDance**, or by calling the following:

800-747-4457 . . . . .U.S. customers
800-465-7301 . . . . .Canadian customers
+44 (0) 113 255 5665 . . . . European customers
08 8372 0999 . . . . Australian customers
0800 222 062 . . . . .New Zealand customers
217-351-5076 . . . . .International customers

For technical support, send an e-mail to:
support@hkusa.com . . . . U.S. and international customers
info@hkcanada.com . . . . Canadian customers
academic@hkeurope.com . . . . European customers
keycodesupport@hkaustralia.com . . . Australian and New Zealand customers

HUMAN KINETICS
The Information Leader in Physical Activity & Health

01-2014

Product: Complete Guide to Primary Dance, w

Key code: PAINE-QYF6YB-OSG

CM005452532

This unique code allows you access to the web resource.

Access is provided if you have purchased a new book. Once submitted, the code may not be entered for any other user.

HUMAN KINETICS WEB RESOURCE

Complete Guide to

PRIMARY DANCE

Lyn Paine

National Dance Teachers Association

HUMAN KINETICS

Library of Congress Cataloging-in-Publication Data

Paine, Lyn.
  Complete guide to primary dance / Lyn Paine, The National Dance Teachers Association.
    pages cm
  Includes bibliographical references.
  1. Dance--Study and teaching (Primary) 2. Dance--Curricula. 3. Movement education. I. Title.
  GV1589.P35 2014
  372.86'8--dc23

2013032666

ISBN-10: 1-4504-2850-9 (print)
ISBN-13: 978-1-4504-2850-7 (print)

The web addresses cited in this text were current as of October 2013, unless otherwise noted.

Acquisitions Editor: Chris Wright; **Developmental Editor:** Jacqueline Eaton Blakley; **Assistant Editors:** Anne Rumery and Bianca Teixeira; **Copyeditor:** Jan Feeney; **Permissions Manager:** Dalene Reeder; **Graphic Designer:** Joe Buck; **Graphic Artist:** Yvonne Griffith; **Cover Designer:** Jonathan Kay; **Photograph (cover):** Pete Millson © Human Kinetics; **Photographs (interior):** Photos on pages 1, 41, 76, 81 (photos 1.1, 4.3, 6.7, 7.6, 8.1) courtesy of NDTA/Photographer: Brian Slater, photos on pages 88, 90, 75 (upper), 84, 51, 55, 56, 30 (left), 31, 47, 17, 22, 29, 51, 2, 3 (upper), 7 (photos 1.2, 1.3, 1.7, 2.3, 2.6, 3.1, 3.2, 3.4, 4.4, 5.1, 7.4, 8.3, 8.6, 8.7) courtesy of Youth Dance England/Photographer: Brian Slater, photos on pages 3 (lower), 4, 6, 18, 20, 30, 32, 34, 39, 75 (lower) 93, 94 (photos 1.4, 1.5, 1.6, 2.4, 2.5, 3.5, 3.6, 4.2, 6.8, 7.5, 9.1, 9.2) © Worcestershire County Council/Photographer: Sue Farr photos on pages 15, 16, 31, 36, 52, 53, 54, 62, 64, 67, 68, 71, 72, 73, 83, 86, 95, 97, (photos 2.1, 2.2, 3.3, 4.1 5.2, 5.3, 5.4, 6.1, 6.2, 6.3, 6.4, 6.5, 7.1, 7.2, 7.3, 8.2, 8.4, 9.2, 9.3) courtesy of Pete Millson © Human Kinetics; **Art Manager:** Kelly Hendren; **Associate Art Manager:** Alan L. Wilborn; **Illustrations:** © Human Kinetics; **Printer:** Versa Press

Printed in the United States of America

10 9 8 7 6 5 4 3 2 1

The paper in this book is certified under a sustainable forestry program.

Human Kinetics
Website: www.HumanKinetics.com

United States: Human Kinetics
P.O. Box 5076
Champaign, IL 61825-5076
800-747-4457
e-mail: humank@hkusa.com

Canada: Human Kinetics
475 Devonshire Road Unit 100
Windsor, ON N8Y 2L5
800-465-7301 (in Canada only)
e-mail: info@hkcanada.com

Europe: Human Kinetics
107 Bradford Road
Stanningley
Leeds LS28 6AT, United Kingdom
+44 (0) 113 255 5665
e-mail: hk@hkeurope.com

Australia: Human Kinetics
57A Price Avenue
Lower Mitcham, South Australia 5062
08 8372 0999
e-mail: info@hkaustralia.com

New Zealand: Human Kinetics
P.O. Box 80
Torrens Park, South Australia 5062
0800 222 062
e-mail: info@hknewzealand.com

E5706

Contents

The Elements of Dance

	BODY	ACTION	SPACE	TIME	ENERGY
Ask:	WHO?	DOES WHAT?	WHERE?	WHEN?	HOW?
Answer:	A dancer	moves	through space	and time	with energy

Concepts (in **bold** font) with some suggestions for word lists and descriptors under each concept.

BODY

Parts of the Body
Head, eyes, torso, shoulders, fingers, legs, feet, etc.

Whole Body
Design and use of the entire body

Initiation
Core
Distal
Mid-limb
Body Parts

Patterns
Upper/lower body, homologous, contralateral, midline, etc.

Body Shapes
Symmetrical/Asymmetrical
Rounded
Twisted
Angular
Arabesque

Body Systems
Muscles
Bones
Organs
Breath
Balance
Reflexes

Inner Self
Senses
Perceptions
Emotions
Thoughts
Intention
Imagination

ACTION

Axial *(in place)*
Open - - - - - - - - - Close
Rise - - - - - - - - Sink or Fall
Stretch - - - - - - - Bend
Twist - - - - - - - - Turn

Laban Effort Actions
Press — Flick
Wring — Dab
Slash — Glide
Punch — Float

Traveling *(locomotor)*
Crawl, creep, roll, scoot, walk, run, leap, jump, gallop, slide, hop, skip, do-si-do, chainé turns ....and many more!

This is just a starting list of movements. Many techniques have specific names for similar actions. "Sauté" is a ballet term for "jump."

SPACE

Place
In Place - - - - - - - Traveling

Size
Small - - - - - - - - - Large

Level
High - - - - - - - - - Low

Direction
Forward - - - - - - Backward
Upward - - - - - - Downward
Sideward - - - - - Diagonally
Liner - - - - - - - Rotating

Pathway
Traveling, traced in air
curved, straight, angular, zig-zag, etc.

Plane
Sagittal (Wheel)
Vertical (Door)
Horizontal (Table)

Focus
Direct - - - - - - - Indirect
Inward - - - - - - - Outward

Relationships
In Front - - - Behind/Beside
Over - - - - - - - Under
Alone - - - - - Connected
Near - - - - - - - Far
Individual & group proximity to object

TIME

Duration
Brief - - - - - - - - - Long

Speed
Fast - - - - - - - - - Slow

Beat
Steady - - - - - - - Uneven

Tempo
Quick - - - - - - - - Slow

Accent
Single - - - - - - - Multiple
On Beat - - - - - Syncopated
Predictable--Unpredictable

Rhythmic Pattern
Patterned - - - - - - Free
Metric
2/4, 6/8, etc
Polyrhythms
Cross-rhythm
Tāla
Breath, waves, word cues, event cues, felt time

Timing Relationships
Before
After
Unison
Sooner Than
Faster Than

ENERGY

Attack
Sharp - - - - - - - Smooth
Sudden - - - - - - Sustained

Tension
Tight - - - - - - - - Loose

Force
Strong - - - - - - - Gentle

Weight
Heavy - - - - - - - Light
Strength: push, horizontal, impacted
Lightness: resist the down, initiate up
Resiliency: rebound, even up and down

Flow
Bound (Controlled) - - Free

Energy Qualities
Vigorous, languid, furious, melting, droopy, wild, lightly, jerkily, sneakily, timidly, proudly, sharp, smooth, sudden, sustained etc.

CHAPTER 8 Dance and the Curriculum · · · 81

CHAPTER 9 Resources for Dance · · · 93

Foreword

The National Dance Teachers Association (NDTA), working in partnership with Human Kinetics, welcomes this exciting new publication, *Complete Guide to Primary Dance*. Lyn Paine is a highly experienced dance practitioner and educator with a wealth of experience in primary education. As a result she has produced an invaluable resource, tool kit and reference guide to support all those involved in teaching dance to children from 4 to 11 years old. It is appropriate for both experienced and non-specialist teachers and those wishing to increase their knowledge and skills.

Complete Guide to Primary Dance provides a framework for creating, performing and watching dances, with an excellent insight into how teachers can plan and manage their dance curriculum. A wealth of stimulating ideas, units of work and strong cross-curricular links will assist teachers in ensuring that all young people in their care will have access to and participate in a high-quality dance experience.

This comprehensive book and web resource encourages the development of creativity, an aspiration for excellence in dance education and creative approaches to teaching and learning. It celebrates dance and we believe that all those who use it will have a valuable resource to inform their work with children and young people for the future.

Judy Evans and Sue Trotman
Joint Chair, NDTA

Preface

Dance is a unique curriculum subject in that it is both physical and expressive. This is what makes it similar to and different from other physical activities and art forms. With its own body of knowledge and clear progression in skills, dance is no "soft" option. By the end of the primary phase, children should be able to lead warm-up and cool-down activities; perform various styles of dances fluently and with control; perform confidently and expressively; demonstrate musicality; adapt and refine the way they use space, dynamics and relationships; work creatively and imaginatively to compose solos, duos and group dances; use appropriate vocabulary to describe, evaluate and reflect on their own and others' dances; talk about dance with understanding; and recognise that dance makes them healthy. In addition, they should have experience in using a range of stimuli (starting points) for dance; dancing to a range of accompaniment; viewing and experiencing dances of various times, places and types; and viewing professional dance live or on film. A good dance education provides young people with the skills and interests to follow a range of vocational and academic pathways and employment opportunities as they grow.

Dance contributes to a balanced physical education programme; it also relates closely to and shares a common language with music, drama and art. Dance can also support learning across the curriculum by bringing stories and poems to life in literacy and by enhancing learning across a range of topics such as those in science and humanities. In lessons and extracurricular activities (dance is second only to football in popularity in UK schools), it promotes physical and mental health and well-being, and those few minutes of fame—the thrill of dancing in front of an audience of family and friends—will be treasured and remembered for the rest of their lives. Dance is both a powerful and empowering experience whether we are participating as performers, choreographers or the audience. No need for fancy gimmicks or equipment—the body is the instrument and movement is the medium. All that is needed is a space in which to dance.

Dance as a curriculum subject can be vulnerable in that many teachers lack the necessary training and there are few resources to support teaching and learning. I have lost count of the number of times that I have been asked, "What sort of dancing do you teach?" as if there were a type or style that is unique to schools. Plenty of promotion, advocacy and broadcasting are still to be done. *Complete Guide to Primary Dance* provides teachers, teaching assistants and dance leaders with a firm knowledge base and the confidence to plan and deliver quality learning experiences that are appropriate to the age and stage of pupils. This book and web resource package is full of practical and creative ideas that will inspire and refresh even the most experienced dance teacher. It is also well suited for dance novices, explaining dance concepts and vocabulary in ways that are easy to understand.

The first three chapters of the book provide theoretical subject knowledge, starting with a discussion about the fundamental nature of dance in chapter 1. Chapter 2 takes a look at the history of dance in education in England over the last 100 years and introduces the model for dance in education that is widely used today. Chapter 3 outlines the key ingredients of dance.

The chapters that follow introduce subject knowledge for teaching (in other words, the subject pedagogy, or how to teach dance). Chapter 4 takes the reader through the processes of planning and teaching and includes a useful section on choreographic knowledge for the teacher. Chapter 5 focuses on warming up and cooling down and includes some very important safe practice content. Chapters 6 and 7 will be of particular interest to teachers who are new to dance or new to teaching because they focus on managing the learning and on assessing dance in relation to current good practice. Chapter 8 looks at the ways in which dance enhances and enriches the curriculum, and the final chapter introduces a wide range of resources for dance.

The book is full of practical ideas and suggestions as well as tasks for teachers that may be used in staff meetings and training sessions, for discussions with students, or for personal reflection. A glossary is included to provide ready reference for unfamiliar terms.

The accompanying web resource exemplifies good practice and demonstrates progression in skills. It is full of material that applies and complements the teaching instruction in the book. It includes the following:

- A complete scheme of work (22 units of work for use with each age of the primary phase) and a template for creating your own dance unit

- Stories, poems, and other written resources that supplement the dances explored in select units
- Video clips that demonstrate many phases of the dance-making process, from selecting ideas for dances to performing a dance
- Photos that illustrate various parts of the dance-making process
- Warm-up activities

This publication was written in the UK and is based on the English education system and curriculum. *Reception* refers to the first year of primary education where children are 4 to 5 years old. *Key Stage 1* (Years 1 and 2) includes children who are 5 to 7 years old, and *Key Stage 2* (Years 3 to 6) includes children who are 7 to 11 years old.

The book and web resource draw on and complement materials and strategies developed by NDTA's partner organisations, who hold a clear vision for dance education and its potential for developing young people's well-being and enhancing their lives.

Lyn Paine

How to Use This Book and Web Resource

This book and web resource work together to offer you a complete guide to teaching dance at the primary level. The book educates you on the teaching of dance from a conceptual viewpoint, and the web resource equips you to put those concepts to work in the classroom with unit plans, warm-ups, written resources, photos and video clips. Throughout the text, when web resource content is referenced, you will see the following icon: ▶

Unit Plans and Scheme of Work

Twenty-two unit plans are organized according to age group (four units for Reception, six for Years 1 and 2, six for Years 3 and 4 and six for Years 5 and 6). The dance ideas in these units will provide teachers with the confidence to deliver dance, supported by the subject knowledge and tools in the book. The units together form a broad, balanced and progressive scheme of work for use from Reception to Year 6. They represent a range of dance ideas, stimuli and types and styles of dance and each focuses on the development of specific skills.

Apart from those for Reception, the units are generally suitable for the two years suggested, which would allow three units per year group. Those planned for Reception could also be used for Year 1, depending on the age and experience of the children. Having several units to select from allows teachers flexibility to decide which units are most suitable for their class and which units support important cross-curricular dimensions. If more than one teacher in the school uses the scheme it is important to plan together to avoid duplication. Ideally dance should be provided regularly in blocks throughout the year—for instance, three six-week or half-term blocks alternating with gymnastics. One unit could be used per block, which allows for one or two short one-off lessons to provide contrast, explore different ideas or focus on specific skills.

Each unit of work includes the following sections:

- **Learning outcomes:** Using all the units for the age groups suggested will enable the children to meet the appropriate expectations for performance, composition and appreciation (see chapter 7: Assessment). Three learning outcomes (usually one each for performing, composing and appreciating) that are specific to each unit have been identified in each unit, although in fact the children will meet several others as well.

- **Stimulus, resources and accompaniment:** Each unit lists at least one stimulus that can spark ideas for dance. Some units of work will have resources that are specific to them, such as a story or a video clip, that are included on the web resource. Other relevant resources and the type of accompaniment (with examples where appropriate) are recommended as well.

- **Dance content:** This section details the key action, dynamic, spatial and relationship content. This information will be helpful in assessing whether the unit will meet the children's needs and enable them to progress.

- **Warm-up:** Warm-up activities (general or specific) suitable for the dance idea are suggested, and sometimes introductory tasks are offered.

- **Assessment:** Assessment opportunities are detailed throughout each unit in the Tasks section, and the Assessment section at the beginning of each unit provides a summary of the relevant assessment strategies. It is strongly recommended that individual achievement in relation to the specific learning outcomes is assessed at the end of each unit. This can be done simply by creating a grid of the children's names and the specific learning outcomes and using traffic lights (red, amber or green) to indicate the level of achievement for each child against each outcome. Specific comments about individuals could also be noted.

- **Curriculum links:** Links to other curriculum areas, topics and themes are provided.

- **Options:** Suggestions for simplifying tasks or providing further challenge are given where appropriate, as well as additional tasks and related activities that may add variety and expand possibilities.

- **Possible unit structure:** Each unit represents a medium-term plan comprising between three and five lessons. There are no individual lesson plans because lesson lengths vary from school to school and age group to age group; also, children's needs vary. However, each unit plan gives an indication of the content for single lessons. Chapter 4: From Ideas to Dances provides clear guidance for lesson planning. Learning outcomes for each lesson can be developed from the unit's specific learning outcomes and from the expectations detailed in chapter 7.

- **Possible dance structure:** Each unit leads to a finished class dance that is likely to comprise some short partner or group sections. To give the dance form, sections might be organised in a different order from that in which they were created. The possible dance structure gives an idea of what the finished dance might look like but is not prescriptive—teachers and children might have other, better ideas!

- **Tasks:** This column details the learning in chronological order. It refers to what the children will do in terms of performing, composing and appreciating dance.

- **Teaching points:** The teaching points add detail to, and are aligned with, each task. They indicate to the teacher what to look for, what to emphasise, how to develop the movement material and how to provide challenge. The criteria for self- and peer assessment are suggested in this column.

Ideally, having used some of these units successfully, teachers will feel inspired and confident, which will encourage them to explore different stimuli, develop their own ideas and plan their own units. To that end, a unit template is provided so that teachers may follow the formula used in these units to plan their own units. Finally, a scheme of work overview gives "at a glance" information about each unit.

Warm-Ups and Written Resources

Written resources include stories and a poem that serve as stimuli for some of the units of work. These could be distributed to students or posted in the dance environment to serve as prompts for the ingredients of dance.

Several warm-up activities are included that are easy to follow and effective. These activities include suggested age groups, recommendations for accompaniment, and step-by-step instructions to lead children through engaging movements that prepare their bodies and minds for dance.

Photos and Video

The photos shown in the book are reproduced on the web resource in full colour. These images may be downloaded for presentations or printed and posted in visual displays, anywhere they might inspire and instruct.

The video section features clips that illustrate various parts of the dance-making process, from conception to performance. These clips will be of value in training sessions and staff meetings when considering teaching and learning strategies and progression. The subfolders in the video section include the following content:

- **Year 2:** Here we follow Year 2 children through the process of creating a dance for the *Tiddalik* unit, inspired by an Aboriginal myth. Video extracts show how the dance idea was developed: the teacher sharing the story with the class, the children exploring movement material and groups of children working to develop their ideas. Finally, we view the performance of a complete dance.

- **Year 4:** In similar fashion as Year 2, here we see extracts that show Year 4 children developing a dance for the *Umbrellas* unit. Select clips of the development process are included along with the performance of a complete dance.

- **Year 6:** The units for Years 5 and 6 are illustrated by video clips of Year 6 children demonstrating several short phrases from a number of units for all age groups that encompass a variety of dance styles.

This book and web resource package is full of material for teaching dance that reflects the expertise of the authors and has been tested and refined in many primary classrooms. Regardless of your current level of experience or comfort with dance, you can be sure that this rich package equips you to be an effective teacher of dance for primary-aged children.

Acknowledgments

Grateful thanks go to the team at Human Kinetics for helping me to realise this book and resource, especially Jackie Blakley for her unfailing humour, enthusiasm and reassurance. Thanks to all at NDTA for having faith in me, especially to Sue Trotman for her support and down-to-earth advice every step of the way. I am indebted to my good friend Sue Cottam for diligently proofreading every word and for her advice and honest feedback. Thanks also to Penny Perrett for her help with the units of work and to other colleagues who have cast their eyes over specific chapters of the book. I am most grateful to all those who have contributed the lovely photos and I applaud photographers Sue Farr, Pete Millson and Brian Slater for their skill in capturing the moment. The children and teachers at St Michael's Primary CE School in Bournemouth were a pleasure to work with—I thank them for giving me time and space during such a busy and pressured term. Finally, I must thank all the children, young people, teachers and colleagues who have inspired me throughout my dance teaching career.

Why Dance?

Dance is vital, an activity both exhilarating and liberating to watch or do. The instinct to dance is fundamentally joyous and no matter how hard you try you can't get away from that for long. It can also be a huge force for good, effectively drawing people together and levelling everyone through sheer hard work. It can speed up your heart rate, it can enliven your being, it can change your life.

Richard Alston, CBE, choreographer and director (Dance UK 2006)

This chapter provides a context for dance in education by exploring the nature of dance, what makes it unique, the benefits of dance, how dance relates to physical education and the arts and what a good dance education will achieve. Dance is both a powerful and empowering means of expression. No one can fail to be moved by a group of primary school children immersed in the moment, believing in themselves, trusting each other and using the full extent of their physical skills and energy as they transport themselves and the audience to an imaginary world in which the impossible can happen.

What Is Dance and What Makes It Unique?

Dance is a fundamental means of human expression. It requires no equipment apart from the body itself (the instrument) and a space in which to move (the medium). We read body language before we listen to what is said. This is why dance, with its non-verbal communication and symbolic movement, affects the viewer immediately.

The uniqueness of dance lies partly in its dual nature—it is both physical and expressive, and this makes it both similar to and different from other physical activities and art forms. Dance develops physical, creative, imaginative,

Dance is a powerful and empowering means of communication.

emotional and intellectual capacities. It also requires social skills. Dance provides opportunities for artistic and aesthetic education as well as opportunities for children to explore and express moods and ideas symbolically through movement. To be physically proficient, children develop a range of technical skills and the ability to improve their performance. Because of its close relationship with music, dance develops rhythmic and musical sensitivity. Through experiencing dance, children can also develop their cultural and historical knowledge and understanding.

Dance has its own body of knowledge, understanding and skills. This is accessed through the processes of performing, composing and appreciating. By the end of the primary phase, children should be able to do the following:

Dance develops coordination, control and strength.

- Lead warm-up and cool-down activities.
- Perform various styles of dance with fluency and control.
- Dance confidently and expressively.
- Perform with musicality.
- Adapt and refine the way they use space, dynamics and relationships.
- Work creatively and imaginatively to create solos, duos and group dances.
- Use appropriate vocabulary to describe, evaluate and reflect on their own and others' dances.
- Talk about dance with understanding.
- Recognise that dance makes them healthy.

In addition, they should have experienced the following:

- A range of starting points and stimuli
- A range of accompaniment
- Dances of different times and places
- Different types of dance
- Viewing professional dance live or on film

Benefits of Dance

Dance has so many significant benefits that daily doses should be prescribed for all!
Artistically, dance

- gives access to a unique form of communication and expression;

- develops the ability to make informed and critical judgements;
- develops creative thought and action;
- develops a sense of performance and audience;
- provides opportunities for appreciating and collaborating with other art forms;
- introduces children to a theatre art; and
- develops kinaesthetic, spatial and visual awareness.

Physically, dance

- develops coordination, control, strength, stamina, mobility and flexibility;
- develops technical skills such as those required for travelling, jumping and turning;
- encourages physical confidence and enjoyment in moving;
- develops a responsible attitude to health and fitness; and
- helps make connections between physical and emotional well-being.

Personally, dance

- provides enjoyment, motivation, aspiration and achievement;
- develops self-confidence and self-esteem;
- develops the ability to respond creatively to challenge;
- provides opportunities to explore links between feelings, values and ideas;

Dance promotes physical trust and sensitivity.

- encourages independence and initiative;
- develops the determination to succeed; and
- provides opportunities for achievement and success for all.

Socially, dance

- promotes physical and emotional trust and sensitivity when working with others;
- develops skills to work with others to solve problems and achieve goals;
- develops the ability to lead and be led and to take on different roles (performer, choreographer, audience);
- provides the opportunity to contribute ideas and share in the creative process; and
- develops the ability to discuss, negotiate, listen and give and receive feedback.

Key Skills

Dance also plays a role in developing a broad range of personal, learning and thinking skills that help children improve their learning and performance in school and life. Some of these skills are explored in more detail in chapter 8. They include the following:

- **Communication:** Children can practise their speaking and listening skills by lis-

tening, understanding and responding to others when creating dances with others. Dance enriches children's use of language when they describe, interpret and evaluate their own and others' dances and respond to the written word when text is used as a stimulus for dance.

- **Application of numbers:** Dance provides opportunities to rehearse mathematical language, particularly space, shape and direction.

- **Information technology:** Digital and video cameras are instrumental in recording and evaluating (and improving) dance. We also use computers and DVDs to view and research dance.

- **Teamwork:** Dance is the perfect medium for developing this skill. To dance effectively with others, children will contribute ideas, meet challenges, collaborate and cooperate. They have to understand the needs and experiences of others and share space sensitively.

- **Self-improvement:** This skill is clearly embedded in the ability to reflect on, evaluate and identify ways to improve performance and composition.

- **Problem solving:** In dance, children translate ideas into actions: this in itself is a problem-solving activity. They have to find ways to find solutions to physical problems such as how to represent a machine with moving parts using four dancers. They also adapt skills and techniques to suit different outcomes, for instance by combining two short partner dances to create a group dance.

Sharing space sensitively.

- **Creative thinking:** This is a fundamental skill for dance composition. It requires the ability to respond imaginatively to a stimulus or idea, explore movements and improvise, generate new movement material and extend and develop material.
- **Independent enquiry:** This is exercised when children plan dances, make informed decisions and explore issues or events from a different perspective.
- **Self-management:** In dance, children are expected to take responsibility for their actions (literally!) and show initiative and perseverance. They also take imaginative risks and show mental flexibility. If they have the desire to improve and the drive to become a better dancer, then they need to manage their emotions and deal with pressure.
- **Effective participation:** Through participating in a range of dance activities, children can play a full part in the life of the school.

Dance and Culture

All dances have a cultural context in that they reflect something of the time and place in which they were created. Dance defines communities and cultures, but it can also transcend them by bringing groups of people from those communities and cultures together. This is because as a form of non-verbal communication it shares a universal language of movement.

Dances of other times and places can be a rich resource from which teachers and children can draw ideas and movement content (see chapter 9). Popular dance styles can provide movement material and are often a good place to start. How-

Task

How would you describe your dance heritage? What is your experience of dance in education and recreation? Which cultural influences have contributed to your dance experience?

ever, it is important not to limit children's experience to one style of dance but to expand their horizons. A rich diet of styles and types of dance will result in a high-quality dance experience. Dance in school is often labelled "creative dance" because it focuses on dances created by the children. These develop from movement exploration and improvisation that could be linked to various dance forms and a range of ideas, topics and themes, or it can simply be based on movement itself. Children who experience dance regularly in school will recognise the relationship between what they do in school and the world of dance beyond that.

Participating in dance in the curriculum and as an extracurricular activity, viewing professional dance (whether live or on video) and participating in workshops and residencies led by visiting dance artists all contribute to the cultural entitlement for all children and young people. Such activities forge effective links between schools, communities, local resources, dance artists and regional organisations and open children's eyes to the world of dance.

Inclusive Practice

Everyone and anyone can dance. The community dance movement, which has grown in Britain over the past 40 or so years, aims to ensure that any person, regardless of age, sex, ability or disability, can access dance activities. There are a growing number of amateur and professional inclusive dance companies such as Candoco (comprising disabled and non-disabled dancers) whose mission is to create a major change in attitudes to dance and disability. Three issues that may affect dance provision in the primary school are disability, gender and faith. Knowledge of the subject and of the children in your care will ensure that you can meet the needs of all children and promote the entitlement to dance for all. You also need to articulate both the nature of dance in education and the benefits it brings. Chapter 6 includes strategies for teaching inclusive dance.

Dances of other times and places provide a rich resource.

Following are actions that address issues of inclusion:

- Know your pupils.
- Focus on the quality of the movement and the movement itself.
- Focus on dance making and encourage the children to own their work.
- Articulate and demonstrate the value of dance education.
- Seek professional advice and support.
- Ensure a safe environment (physically and emotionally).
- Build an ethos of support and respect.

Disability

Every class can include students with various physical and cognitive challenges, including learning difficulties, physical disabilities and visual and hearing impairments. Teachers are accustomed to adapting curricula for a range of needs in all subjects, and dance is no exception. Effective dance teachers set tasks that meet individual needs and provide suitable challenge for each child, such as limiting or extending the content of a dance phrase or the group size or providing resources such as visual or verbal prompts to support learners. Further examples of differentiation are provided in chapter 6.

Gender

We sometimes encounter negative attitudes to boys' dancing, but interestingly adults, not the boys, more often hold these attitudes. Dance is a valuable and inclusive activity, and you can promote it as such by providing opportunities for participation and sharing dance processes and outcomes with other children, colleagues and parents or caregivers. Boys are disadvantaged in secondary schools where dance is often available only to girls and most dance teachers are female. The lack of dance education for boys in secondary schools impedes their access to dance beyond school, unfortunately, and is therefore an issue of equal opportunities. Where dance is an entitlement for all young people, there is often evidence of improved behaviour, attendance and achievement.

Faith

In a diverse population, teachers should be sensitive to the varied beliefs and attitudes about dance. Negative attitudes often arise from misconceptions about the kind of dance that schools promote and may stem from a belief that popular

Task

What are the obstacles to inclusion in dance? How might these be overcome?

social dance forms are not morally or spiritually acceptable. As a teacher, you have a responsibility to articulate what you do in dance and why you value it.

Dance Beyond the Classroom

A high-quality dance education will provide young people with the skills and interests to select from and follow a range of recreational, vocational and academic pathways and make informed choices about further study, employment, lifestyles and lifelong learning. This book focuses on dance in the curriculum and provides a systematic and progressive programme, but dance in schools should not be taught in a vacuum. Dance is also a very popular extracurricular activity: Before- and after-school clubs and community programmes attract large numbers of young participants. School dance clubs might focus on a particular style of dance, or they could run for a limited number of sessions in the lead-up to a special event. For children who wish to develop their interest out of school, local and regional dance agencies can provide teachers and parents with information about what's offered in the community.

Young people are exposed daily to the expanding popular dance industry. Commercials, music videos, talent shows and dance films play a significant role in their culture and lives. At the same time, the number and range of academic and vocational courses in secondary schools and colleges have increased significantly, and a growing number of young people study dance in higher education and go on to work in the dance, arts and leisure industries. Young people may also enjoy the social and health benefits of dance classes in the community, and there are expanding opportunities to join youth dance groups and projects.

Dance in the Curriculum

Because of its uniqueness and the benefits it brings, there is no doubt that dance deserves a place in the curriculum. Learning *in* dance is learning to perform, compose and appreciate dance using the distinctive movement vocabulary of dance. Dance is also a valuable medium through which children can access other areas

Task

Research the opportunities in the local community for children to dance and to watch dance. Who could help you signpost the opportunities?

Task

Draw up a document that makes the case to the following people for dance in the curriculum:

- Governors
- Parents
- Colleagues

of the curriculum. We call this learning *through* dance. Dance facilitates the development of key skills and can provide children with a unique kinaesthetic experience in other subjects, for instance by exploring the words and phrases in movement to bring a poem to life in a literacy lesson or by demonstrating the power of the electric circuit in movement.

An effective way of using both learning in and through dance is to plan dance activities alongside other curriculum areas, capitalising on meaningful links and at the same time ensuring progression in skills, knowledge and understanding in dance. Chapter 8 and the scheme of work on the web resource provide more detail.

Dance and the Arts

Dance has a close relationship with the other art forms. Through the arts we explore ideas, create images and form compositions to deal with who we are and the world around us. In the arts we use our senses to explore and make sense of this complex world. In dance we employ the kinaesthetic sense, whereas art requires tactile and visual senses. Music relies on the aural and tactile senses, and drama requires both verbal and kinaesthetic senses. How we make sense of the world depends on our ability to recognise relationships and order patterns.

Dance, like art, is concerned with creating designs in space. Like music, dance shares the dimension of time. Both dance and drama require space and time in which to create and order patterns. Dancers use movement to create statements, whilst other art forms require dexterity and fine motor skills, such as using a paintbrush or playing an instrument, or use of language. In dance the body is the instrument and movement is the medium. Each art form represents a unique way of responding to and making sense of the world through a unique combination of senses

and through a unique medium, which is why one cannot take the place of the other.

The three processes of doing, making and reviewing are common to music, art, drama and, to some extent, poetry and story making. Performing in dance equates with developing skills and techniques in art, using techniques in drama and singing or playing music. Composing in dance is similar to investigating, designing and creating in art and creating in drama and composing in music. Finally, appreciating in dance equates with knowing about the work of artists and designers in art, responding to and evaluating work in drama, and listening, appreciating and understanding in music. Links between dance and the arts are explored further in chapter 8. The arts also share a common vocabulary, predominantly in relation to the compositional process and also in terms of aesthetics. The aesthetic qualities of dance are explored in more detail in chapter 9.

Dance and Physical Education

Dance enjoys a privileged place in the curriculum because it is both artistic and physical. For many years, training in Britain for general pri-

Dance creates designs in space.

mary and secondary PE teaching has included dance, or **modern educational dance** as it was called in the 1950s and '60s. The established position of dance in physical education in the national curriculum of the 1980s has led to many improvements in teaching, learning and provision; national strategies such as the PE and Sport Strategy for Young People have further raised the profile of dance and enabled more primary teachers to deliver dance with confidence. In practical terms, dance provides a balanced activity that contrasts with and complements games, gymnastics, athletics, outdoor and adventure activities and swimming. Dance requires a reasonable space and therefore needs time tabling alongside other activities requiring a similar environment, such as gymnastics. Dance shares characteristics with gymnastics, but the intention and outcome are different. In gymnastics the focus is on skills, agility and fluency in linking and coordinating actions on the floor and on apparatus, and the movement is an end in itself. Dance shares the elements of action, dynamics, space and relationships, but these are used imaginatively to create dances that express ideas and feelings. Here the movement is a means to a different end.

Dance also shares a number of basic motor skills with other physical education activities. **Fundamental movement skills** (FMS) are categorised in three groups: body management, locomotion and object control (or manipulation); many schools focus on the development of these fundamental movement skills in the formative years by using specific programmes or schemes of work to develop children's **physical literacy**. Dance provides a context for developing two of the three FMS categories: body management and locomotion. Body management skills include static and dynamic balances, twisting and turning, bending and stretching, alignment and control in movement and stillness and in changing shape or direction. Locomotor skills include running, hopping, skipping, galloping and jumping. Warm-ups and most other dance activities use both sets of skills. To a lesser extent, dance can also provide a context for practising the third FMS category: manipulation—the controlling of objects with body parts (usually hands and feet). Children could, for instance, explore space using streamers or lengths of material to show the movements of fire or water, or they could replicate a machine's moving parts and the process of manufacturing by passing a basketball from one player to the other in a machine-like way.

The thrill of jumping!

The key activities or processes of performing, composing and appreciating dance have clear links to key aspects of learning in physical education: acquiring skills; applying skills, tactics and compositional ideas; and evaluating and improving performance. On the whole, the language of physical education is objective and scientific, and the language of dance tends to have more in common with other art forms.

Task

Think about the relationship between dance and physical education. What is the difference between dance and gymnastics? Why is dance not an Olympic sport? What makes dance an artistic activity? What are the advantages and disadvantages of including dance as part of physical education?

High-Quality Dance Outcomes

Given a regular and progressive dance education, what should we expect of a dance-educated child at the age of 11? In 2005 the National Dance Teachers Association, together with representatives from the Department for Culture, Media and Sport, Youth Dance England and QCA, took the 10 high-quality outcomes for physical education and school sport established by the PESSCL (PE, School Sport and Club Links) strategy to develop specific dance outcomes in a publication titled *Dance Links: A Guide to Delivering High Quality Dance for Children and Young People.* The dance outcomes are in table 1.1, along with what each might look like in practice at the age of 11.

Table 1.1 High-Quality Dance Outcomes

When schools and clubs provide high-quality dance, young people	We can see this when children
1. are **committed** to dance and keen to experience a range of dance through participation, observation and discussion.	• are positive, enthusiastic and cooperative; • are interested in watching dance and willing to talk about dance; and • practise dances and take some responsibility for their own work.
2. know and **understand** what they wish to achieve in a range of dance forms from different cultural contexts.	• have some understanding of different styles and forms of dance.
3. appreciate the benefits of dance as part of a **healthy active lifestyle** and are able to make choices about its role in their lives.	• understand the need to and how to warm up and cool down and the effect on the body; and • know that dance is a healthy option.
4. have **confidence** in their own dance activities and have high self-esteem.	• offer ideas and create their own and group dances; • perform with commitment; and • talk about their own and others' work and give feedback.
5. demonstrate increased **skills** and physical competence in dance.	• extend their movement range; • perform with clarity of actions, space and dynamics; • remember movement patterns and dances; • perform with musicality; and • show sensitivity to other dancers.
6. create and perform dances that communicate an artistic intention using a **range** of dance styles.	• respond imaginatively to stimuli and starting points; • are willing to explore and experiment with movement; • select movement material appropriate to the dance idea; • create and structure dances; • consider spatial design; • communicate the dance idea successfully; and • use accompaniment appropriately.
7. **think** critically about dance and communicate effectively about their own and others' work, including professional dance works.	• describe, analyse, interpret and evaluate dance using appropriate vocabulary; • link movement to meaning; • reflect on own and others' work; and • give and receive feedback.
8. **show a desire to improve** in dance and celebrate their dance experiences through a range of activities including performances.	• rehearse and practise to improve performance; • pay attention to detail; and • act on feedback.

When schools and clubs provide high-quality dance, young people	We can see this when children
9. have the **stamina, suppleness and strength** to participate in dance, understanding and applying aspects of safe dance practice.	• show respect for themselves and others; • take responsibility for warming up and cooling down; • are flexible, move with control and keep going; • sit, stand and move well with good posture and alignment; • do not give up or drop out easily; and • control their breathing.
10. **enjoy** dance and are engaged and motivated whilst dancing.	• engage with dance and look happy; • ask questions; • are eager for new experiences; • take part in extracurricular activities; • enjoy opportunities to watch dance; and • are keen to perform and compose dances.

Task

Reflect on and discuss with colleagues what is needed in your school in order to achieve the 10 high-quality dance outcomes. Can you add 2 more to the list?

Summary

Dance is a fundamental form of human expression. The universal language of movement plays a key role in joining communities and transcending cultures. Dance brings about many benefits including artistic, physical, personal, social and key skills. Everyone can dance regardless of ability, gender and faith. Those who are involved with dance in education will be familiar with its many benefits. We are also acutely aware of its vulnerability in schools and in the community; hence the need to articulate and demonstrate the values of dance to the wider public.

The Dance Model

This chapter introduces the model for dance in education by considering how dance has evolved in schools in England since the start of the 20th century. The chapter explores the three activities of performing, composing and appreciating that underpin teaching and learning in dance and highlights how these can be integrated in practice.

Brief History of Dance in Education

A concern for children's health and physical condition underpinned *The Syllabus of Physical Exercises for Schools* (HMSO 1909), the aim of which was to achieve sound character, an active intelligence and a healthy physique. The syllabus proposed that the introduction of dancing steps would lead to enjoyment, freedom and exhilaration, although the physical education content was delivered as progressive sequences of exercises and commands from the teacher. Dancing was seen to promote a graceful carriage, balance and control and was viewed as recreational and natural. Dances that expressed joy and spirit, such as Morris dances, jigs and reels, were recommended. For infant classes, short and varied lessons with scope for free movements were proposed together with simple and rhythmic exercises accompanied by music to increase enjoyment.

By 1933, dance enjoyed the same status as swimming and athletics in the school curriculum. *The Syllabus for Physical Training* (HMSO 1933) continued to recognise that healthy physical growth was essential to intellectual growth, and short daily lessons of physical training, preferably in the open air, were recommended. Dance, a stimulating, enjoyable and rhythmic activity involving harmonious movement of the whole body, was delivered in most girls' and infant departments and was gaining ground for boys. In the early stages dance movements would be based on walking, running, hopping and skipping to simple melodies, and for older children preliminary exercises would be followed

by learning set dances from the folk and national repertoire of England, Scotland and Europe. Infant departments were also encouraged to develop imagination and drama through action songs, singing games and familiar stories, providing that the resulting movement was worthwhile!

The picture in 1952 changed somewhat with the emphasis swinging from performing set dances to creating dances. "Moving and Growing" (part 1 of *Physical Education in the Primary School*; HMSO 1952), which replaced the 1933 syllabus for physical training, emphasised the need for exploration and creation. It focused on ways of learning, the different ages and stages of children and gender differences. The photographs in "Moving and Growing" show bare-chested and barefoot children swinging, climbing and leaping in indoor and outdoor environments. In the 1950s movement and dance were viewed as art forms that arose from an overflow of feeling, energy or excitement. Movement was to be enjoyed for its own sake, and the quality, shape and pattern were important elements. The children were the artists and it was the teacher's role to provide material to stimulate imagination and help shape ideas. The book distinguishes between adult dances (social and traditional) and children's created dances. "Moving and Growing" also recognised the value of dramatic movement, which was stimulated by both real and imagined experience and transformed emotion into physical form.

Laban's Model

Rudolf Laban (1879–1958) made a significant contribution to dance in education in Britain in the 1950s and '60s. His approach to modern educational dance significantly influenced the training of primary teachers and secondary PE teachers for many years to follow. Laban, a Hungarian, was inspired by the European modern dance movement of the 1920s and 1930s. He established movement choirs of untrained dancers and choreographed dances for the opening of the Berlin Olympic Games. Laban fled to Britain soon after, where he concentrated on the use of movement in industrial settings (thus supporting the war effort) and modern educational dance. Laban's interests in the relationship between body, space and effort and of types and directions of movement provided the basis for Laban notation, which consists of graphic symbols for body parts, actions, space, time and relationships; the notation system is used today for analysing and recording movement and reconstructing dances. Laban's principles of movement underpinned the teaching of modern educational dance and his 16 movement themes linked to stages in the development of the growing child:

1. Body awareness
2. Awareness of force and time
3. Awareness of space
4. Flow of weight in space and time
5. Adapting to a partner
6. Instrumental use of the limbs
7. Isolated actions
8. Occupational rhythms
9. Shapes (pathways in space)
10. Combining the eight basic effort actions
11. Spatial orientation
12. Shapes and efforts
13. Elevation
14. Group feeling
15. Group formations
16. Expressive qualities

Laban believed that every action had a quality (or **effort**), and he focused on the universality of movement. He promoted dance as a natural activity that required an inner attitude to the flow of movement, pervading all of the body, rather than a vocabulary of specific actions. Laban (1948) and his followers believed in children inventing their dances freely. Modern educational dance promoted the beneficial effect of creative activity on the dancer and not the artistic perfection of the dance. Laban's legacy can be summarised as follows:

- He established the Art of Movement Studio in Surrey in 1946, now the Trinity Laban Conservatoire in South East London, which has been influential in training teachers and dancers and fostering new choreographers and dance companies.

- His approach to dance was inclusive and community based.

- His accurate analysis of movement and space underpins the dance content that is taught today, and his notation system has stood the test of time.

- His approach was founded on natural movement of the whole body and required no specific technique.

Smith-Autard's Midway Model

The late 1960s and 1970s saw a growth in contemporary dance in Britain. Establishments such as the London School of Contemporary Dance, influenced by the American modern dance movement, trained dancers who in turn formed touring companies providing workshops for colleges and schools to complement their performances. It was no wonder that the audience for contemporary dance grew. The style was less exclusive than ballet, with techniques grounded in more natural movement, and it employed a broad range of actions and a full use of space. It was unisex and unpretentious and it explored contemporary themes or dealt with classic themes in a contemporary way. The simultaneous growth and popularity of musical theatre and the availability of these forms of dance on video brought dance as theatre art into the lives of many more young people than ever before.

The 1980s saw the introduction of a national curriculum for England and Wales, which included dance as one of the physical education activities, and its popularity grew as a **general certificate of secondary education (GCSE)** subject. During this period the processes of performance, composition and appreciation began to form the common currency for delivering dance in both primary and secondary schools. In 1994 Jacqueline Smith-Autard, a leading British dance educator, proposed a midway model (1994, p. 26) as shown in table 2.1, for dance in education that comprised the best features of Laban's educational (or process) model of the 1950s and '60s and the professional (or product) model promoted in secondary and higher education, which was influenced by American modern dance of the 1970s. This theoretical framework for the art of dance in education, focusing on performance, composition and appreciation, was applicable to primary, secondary and higher education. It represented the consensus of dance education and demonstrated the relationship between creativity, imagination and feelings and the techniques and conventions of dance. It also focused on dance's contribution to artistic, aesthetic and cultural education.

The midway model established a framework for progression through all phases of education in that the three processes of composition, performance and appreciation formed the core around which lessons and the dance curriculum were structured. The experiences of making, perform-

Table 2.1   Midway Model of Dance in Education

Educational	Midway	Professional
Process	Process and product	Product
Creativity	Creativity	Knowledge of theatre dance repertoire
Imagination	Imagination and individuality	
Individuality	Knowledge of public, artistic conventions	
Feelings	Feelings and skill	Skill acquired
Subjectivity	Subjectivity and objectivity	Objectivity
Principles	Principles and techniques	Techniques
Open methods	Open and closed	Closed methods
Creating	Three strands (composition, performance, appreciation) of dances leading to artistic, aesthetic and cultural education	Performing

ing and viewing dances applied to children's own dances or those of their peers, professionals and dancers from different traditions and cultures.

- Performing related to the interpretation of dances showing an understanding of meaning
- Composing related to the translation of ideas into movement
- Appreciating related to perceiving dance and making critical judgements

A simple model of dance that forms the basis of this book can be seen in figure 2.1. The ingredients of dance—actions, dynamics, space and relationships—are the physical elements of movement material that are used in performance, composition and appreciation (i.e., methods used in a cookery theme). Stimuli, accompaniment, styles and types provide the different flavours.

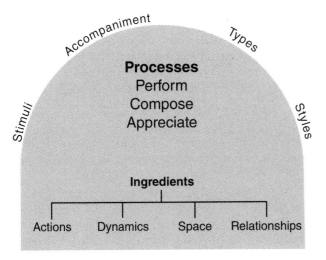

Figure 2.1   A simple model of dance.

Performing

Performing is doing, or dancing. It's unfortunate that the word *performance* is often associated with a polished presentation to an audience, but it is not a bad idea for teachers and children to hold that concept in their minds throughout the dance lesson so that with every task the children do their best. This requires self-discipline and control. There are five dimensions of performing (see figure 2.2):

1. Using technical skills to perform a range of actions, dynamic qualities and dance relationships with spatial awareness
2. Developing a movement memory
3. Using the expressive skills that communicate and enhance the meaning of the dance
4. Developing the skills for presenting dance to an audience (this includes sharing work with peers)
5. Understanding and demonstrating the principles of safe practice in dance

Performance skills develop in relation to the movement vocabulary, which includes a range of actions and dynamic qualities, using various aspects of space and different dance relationships

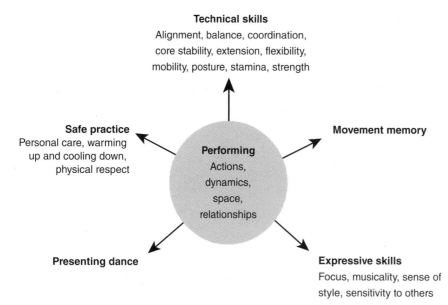

Figure 2.2 Five dimensions of performing.

with others. This dance vocabulary is what children will draw on when composing their dances, and it is explored in detail in chapter 3.

Technical Skills

It is important to understand the **technical skills** necessary for dance, but it is equally important to remember that in schools we are educating children in dance rather than training them to dance. Focus on movements that are natural, safe, efficient and effective, and use common sense when identifying and correcting faults and teaching technical skills. Technical skills will mainly be introduced, practised and developed in the warm-up and introductory tasks of the lesson. Table 5.1 in chapter 5 suggests tasks for improving physical and technical skills.

Good habits underpin effective learning in dance. From the moment children enter the space to the moment they leave, performance skills can be reinforced in expectations for standing and sitting, warming up and cooling down, exploring movements and rehearsing and presenting work. Praising good posture, relaxed shoulders and extended feet will reinforce good practice for all children. Using imagery such as "stretch like a cat" and "spring like a tiger" will help children achieve the appropriate quality of movement. They will also benefit from the modelling of good practice, whether by peers, teachers or a professional dancer on film. Many of the following principles overlap and rely on each other.

Alignment

This is a dynamic state in preparing to move and also in holding shapes. It is concerned with the relationship between parts of the body and, like posture, is vital for efficiency and **aesthetic** appearance. Always remind children of the linear relationship between ears, shoulders, hips, knees and feet when standing tall—there should be a sense of connection. Poor alignment can sometimes be seen in landing from jumps, when bending the knees and when balancing and stretching. Contemporary dance uses both parallel and turned-out positions. Turning out involves rotation of the hip so that the whole leg rotates. The position allows for more freedom and stability, such as in a balance on one leg or a lunge. Some children try to turn out their feet more than their natural hip flexibility allows, which can result in the feet rolling in and can also put stress on the knee joints.

Balance

To achieve balance, a dancer needs a stable base, muscular tension and a sense of connection between body parts. It is easier to achieve balance near the floor when the centre of gravity is low and when the base is wide or uses either a large area of the body or a number of points such as hands and feet. Focusing on a still object in the distance aids balance, but muscular tension is the crucial ingredient. The most challenging balance is on one foot with limbs extended.

Control

This is the ability to start and stop moving, change direction and hold a shape. It relies on muscular tension and awareness of the centre of gravity. Lifting the weight, or pulling up from the centre of the body, can increase control, such as when balancing; on the other hand, keeping the centre of gravity (deep in the pelvis) low can help control speed and change direction, such as when dodging.

Coordination

This is the combination of body parts in action and of actions themselves, which become more complex as children develop. Coordination ranges from the natural (such as swinging arms when walking) to the complex (such as turning and jumping whilst travelling across the floor). Tasks that encourage cross-lateral movements (such as creeping like a tiger or climbing the rigging like a sailor) are important for developing coordination in younger children. Experiencing dances from a range of cultures will provide additional coordination challenges for all.

Core Stability

The muscles involved in achieving this are deep in the pelvic region. Core stability is what helps dancers control movements, achieve balance and change direction and shape. Martha Graham, American modern dance pioneer, considered that all movement emanated from the solar plexus (located in the abdomen at the point of the diaphragm), and she used the energy of the **contraction** and extension of these deep core muscles and the spine as a basis for her technique. Reminding children of the connection between the centre of the body and the limbs will improve control and balance.

Energy flowing through the body in a clear extended shape.

Extension

This is both a physical and expressive performance skill. Good extension is achieved by stretching every muscle in the limbs and sensing the energy flowing through them and out through the extremities. Pointing the toes and stretching the fingers will lengthen the lines of the limbs and the body. Extension is a two-way process that also requires a certain amount of resistance—stretching upwards also requires a firm base with a feeling of pushing into the ground.

Flexibility

Many children are blessed with natural flexibility, and it is important that they maintain and develop flexibility as it increases the range within and across different actions. Flexibility relates to the elasticity of the muscles and the range of mobility in the joints, so warm-up activities that mobilise the joints and stretch the muscles will aid flexibility. Some children can hyperextend their joints, but joints need to be protected by muscular strength as their flexibility could lead to injury as their bodies develop and change.

Mobility

Mobility in dance has two meanings. It can refer to the range of motion in a joint, or it can refer to the ability to move fluently from action to action.

Joint mobility is covered in chapter 5. Fluent movement is possible if children experience a full range of actions (travelling, turning, balancing, jumping and gesturing) and have opportunities to apply different aspects of speed, strength and flow to their actions. They also need to be confident when moving on the floor, along the floor and away from the floor (as in jumping).

Posture

Good posture is vital for both technical and aesthetic reasons. Each section of the body needs to be properly aligned with the other sections in order to achieve efficient and effective movement and to breathe properly. Common faults include slouching and unevenly distributing weight (i.e., placing more weight on one hip than the other when standing).

Stamina

This is the ability to maintain movement over periods of time and involves muscles, heart and lungs. Despite current opinions, children naturally have stamina (watch them at playtime!), and this should be maintained and developed in dance and physical education lessons. Avoiding excessive stops and starts and prolonged periods of sitting and listening to instructions will help. Dance lessons should begin with active aerobic warm-ups of around 3 to 5 minutes to raise heart rate.

Strength

Strength is important for efficient and safe movement, and strong muscles can continue activity for longer. Movement is brought about by muscular contraction with the muscles working in pairs—one contracting and the other lengthening.

A range of tasks for developing and improving physical and technical skills can be found in chapter 5.

Movement Memory

The ability to copy, repeat and remember actions and movement phrases and patterns is fundamental to performing. With the youngest children, the process begins with action rhymes and familiar songs, whilst older children can be expected to learn, remember and perform a dance lasting as long as 5 minutes. It helps, of course, if the children have ownership of the movement material—in other words, if they have created parts of a dance or a whole dance. Warm-up sequences that include repeated or developed patterns of movement, or a chorus, will help develop movement memory. It has been noted that daily physical exercise sessions for children (where the whole school or key stage participate in exercise to music) have made a significant impact on movement memory. Structuring class dances that include a repeated chorus, such as a dance to a rock 'n' roll song, will also aid movement memory as well as musicality. Children enjoy learning and performing movement phrases and dances created by others, such as traditional folk dances, as much as they enjoy creating their own dances, so it is important to achieve a balance of experiences.

Expressive Skills

Just as important as technical skills, expressive skills are what help communicate the dance idea and catch viewers' attention. All children, regardless of their technical skills and physical competence, can develop and achieve good expressive skills. Table 2.2 suggests tasks to use with children for exploring and improving expressive skills.

Focus

Focus is where the dancer looks—it might be up, down, at or beyond the audience. A dancer might also focus on part of the body, such as in Indian dance where the eyes follow the hand, or on another dancer or prop. Good focus draws the viewer to the dancers and also to the meaning of the dance, and it highlights important moments in the dance. It can be both powerful and dramatic. Being focused as a performer is also an important skill. Learning to concentrate on the movement and meaning of the dance and not to be distracted by others, clothing, hair or the audience are all important performance skills. Carrying on when things go wrong is a desirable life skill.

Good focus draws the viewer to the dance.

Projection

Projection is about bringing the meaning or dance idea to life and gives it energy. It connects the dancer to the audience members and helps them understand the meaning. Children should be encouraged to make movements clear and bold where appropriate and to emphasise the dynamic qualities. The technical skill of extension is also an important aspect of projection. Also consider the use of facial expression; if no specific expression is required, the face and eyes should still look alive.

Musicality

Musicality is the ability to use the qualities and features of the accompaniment with sensitivity and accuracy. Musicality involves timing, phrasing and rhythm. Qualities of the accompaniment that can be interpreted in movement are mood, contrast, repetition, climax, rhythm and pulse. A range of types and styles of accompaniment will develop musical sensitivity, as will taking the time to listen to and talk about music. Plenty of practice with accompaniment helps children become familiar with the structure and qualities so they can anticipate moments of climax and contrast and match their movements accordingly.

Sense of Style

Style is both a technical and expressive skill and is about getting inside the dance. It becomes more significant as children grow older, but even the youngest can show stylistic differences between, for instance, African- and Asian-themed dances. The combination of technical and expressive skills is enhanced by a good choice of accompaniment. Read more about styles of dance in chapter 9.

Sensitivity to Others

Dances generally include more than one dancer, and the ability to perform with others is a crucial skill to develop from an early age. Sensitivity to others is about relating movements to those of others in time and space. It requires a responsibility for self and a shared responsibility for others—whether holding hands in a circle or performing a complex partner dance involving contact and weight taking. Good group work requires peripheral vision where dancers are aware of each other without looking directly at them. There is more detail on relationships, contact and weight taking in chapter 3.

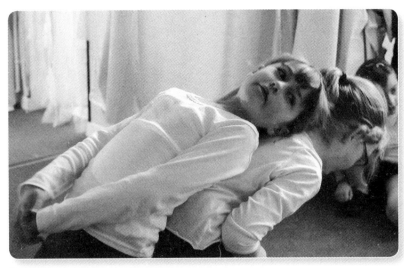
Shared responsibility and sensitivity.

Presenting Dance

Every child deserves an opportunity to perform to an audience, whether it is to another class in the school hall or to a large public audience in a local theatre. Performance in the formal sense raises standards because children will concentrate and focus well, take responsibility, demonstrate independence and try harder. The buzz of excitement and nervous anticipation before the event and the sense of satisfaction and high self-esteem afterwards combine to

Table 2.2 Tasks for Exploring and Improving Expressive Skills

Expressive skill	Tasks
Focus	• Stand still and explore a range of movements led by one hand, following the hand with the eyes. Repeat the task but look straight ahead or at the floor. Watch a partner and evaluate the outcomes. • A group of children focus on a specific point in the distance. They move together towards and away from the focal point—is it mysterious, wonderful, scary, powerful, horrible? Watch and evaluate.
Projection	• Reach forward with both arms. Give one arm extra energy, extension and intensity. Notice the difference. • Look at cartoons or comic strips for different facial expressions. Explore and practise sad, happy, angry, sulky, mischievous and so on. Guess each other's. Add posture, position and action—is it clearer?
Musicality	• Match movements to various percussion sounds to develop listening skills and rhythmic awareness, such as in a warm-up or in a machine dance. • Listen to a short piece of music such as a rock song. Identify introduction, choruses, verses, instrumental sections and ending. What rock 'n' roll movements would work for each section?
Sense of style	• Create a short partner phrase of travelling, turning, meeting and parting. Perform it to 3 different styles of music (hip-hop, courtly and Bhangra). How does each make children feel, and how did they adapt their sequence to suit each musical style?
Sensitivity to others	• In a circle, holding hands, slowly sit then stand without letting go. • Lead a partner (with their eyes closed) carefully around the space. Once confident, vary the speed, direction and level of movement.

provide a unique experience. It is not always necessary to have a formal audience; the experience begins in the dance lesson when children share their work with critical friends. A polished performance could be recorded on video to be shared with the dancers and others. High-quality performance is the result of many factors:

- Effective teamwork
- Determination to improve and succeed
- Resilience
- Ownership of the composition
- Clarity about what is being communicated
- Familiarity with accompaniment
- Clarity about own and others' roles
- Sense of audience

The buzz of performing is a lasting memory.

All this requires opportunities to rehearse, an understanding of what is being aimed for and regular and effective feedback. Encourage the youngest children to copy, create, remember and repeat simple movement phrases and short dances that have clear starting and finishing positions. In her book *Knowing Dance*, Marion Gough (1999, p. 76) notes the following:

> *Beginning is not simply being still—it is about being alert, prepared mentally and physically for what is to follow, focused. Ending is not just a stop—it is about holding on to the clarity of movement, complete stillness, nothing moving, holding the gaze, conclusion.*

Safe Dance Practice

Much of this is covered from a teacher's perspective in chapters 5 and 10. However, this section deals with the children's knowledge, understanding and skills. The following aspects can be introduced and practised from the start so as to establish good lifelong habits.

Personal Care

Children should understand that they need a balanced and healthy diet to supply energy for exercise and dance and that they need to drink plenty of water. They should appreciate that regular dance activity is an effective and enjoyable way to stay healthy. It is also good for children to understand the importance of presenting themselves safely for dance by wearing appropriate clothing, dancing barefoot as a norm, tying back long hair and removing jewellery.

Warming Up and Cooling Down

Children need to know why they warm up and cool down in a dance lesson. The youngest children should be able to explain the effects of exercise on the body, and as they grow they should be able to explain it in more detail as well as design their own warm-up and cool-down sequences.

Physical Respect

Children should learn to respect their own bodies by carrying out movements such as jumping, falling and rolling safely. When jumping, they must learn to land quietly with bent or soft knees and good alignment. When falling, they should let the floor absorb their weight, using successive body parts and spreading their weight along the floor. Rolling requires momentum and a degree of body tension as well as an understanding of shape and body surfaces. They must also learn to respect those with whom they share space, taking responsibility to avoid collisions as they move around and through space and when they use contact and share or take weight. Children need to be aware of their own weight and strength before they can partner with others, and dance provides a safe context for developing physical sensitivity and trust.

Composing

Composing (or choreographing) is about translating ideas into and communicating them through movement. It is by far the most important activity to focus on because it requires both performance and appreciation skills in order to create effective dances. Figure 2.3 shows the composition process and the skills involved.

Chapter 4 explores stimuli and the composition process in more detail. This chapter focuses on the composition skills that children will need to develop and practise in order to create their own dances.

Responding and Exploring

Responding to a stimulus is often a multisensory process, predominantly requiring visual, audio and kinaesthetic responses. In other words, it is about looking at, listening to and feeling the movement. With younger children, touch is also an important sense for responding to a stimulus. You do not need to search far and wide for suitable stimuli for dance because stimuli are often already in the classroom, such as stories, poems, pictures and artefacts that are resources and starting points for a wide range of curriculum areas. Talking about the stimulus or starting point for a dance and suggesting words or phrases for actions, shapes and images could form a bank of movement ideas that might eventually be broader than the actual stimulus.

The quality of your questioning as you discuss the stimulus with children is crucial for eliciting breadth and depth of creative ideas.

Creating and Selecting Material

This is where children try out or explore movements in response to the stimulus. A word bank would support them in translating ideas into movement, and it is always best to begin with **action** words before considering **dynamic** qualities, elements of **space** and dance **relationships**. Children should be confident to create and explore movements, but sometimes they need a few actions modelled for them or to be given a short sequence of actions to play with.

You can encourage the youngest children to make choices, for instance by choosing a starting and finishing position. With a little more experience they can select three actions from a list or choose a character to represent.

Developing Material

Once selected, movements can be developed in a limitless number of ways to create richer material. Children can develop movements by changing

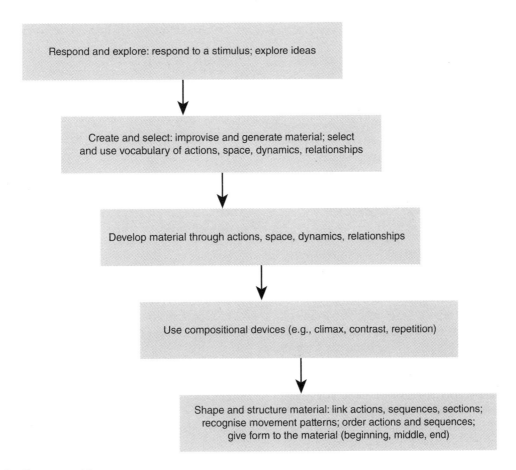

Figure 2.3 The composition process.

Children exploring movements with confidence.

Shaping and Structuring Material

Whether they are linking actions to make short movement phrases or composing a four-minute group dance, children make decisions about the order and overall shape of their dances. By giving movements form and recognising pattern and sequence children set their movement material so that they can remember and repeat it. The primary class dance is often structured so that children contribute their own material to certain sections and might, for instance, include a beginning where all the children perform similar movements as directed by the teacher. They might then perform their partner or group dances (a few at a time). The dance could end with all the children performing a developed version of the starting sequence. Table 2.3 shows how the composition skills are used in dances for different age groups.

Experience of the following will enable children to develop composition skills:

- A range of stimuli and starting points
- Opportunities to participate in structured dances as individuals and in pairs, small groups and large groups
- A range of tasks from directed to open ended
- Ownership of their own ideas and outcomes
- A range of accompaniment
- Different styles and types of dance

They will learn best in a positive environment where creativity is valued and they feel confident to explore and experiment with movement. They also need time to do this in the lesson. They will learn best if you have clear knowledge of the principles of dance composition and are confident in modelling and can provide examples of professional dance on film or in live performance.

Appreciating

Critical appreciation requires a range of skills that are fundamental to good teaching and learning in dance. The skills and understanding of appreciation apply to children's own dances, the work of their peers and dances created and performed by others, including dances of other times and places and professional dance works performed in public places such as theatres or on film (see figure 2.4).

and adding or subtracting aspects of action, space, dynamics and relationships. Children need plenty of practice in developing movement material in order to expand their vocabulary of actions and their knowledge of dynamics, space and relationships. Teacher-directed structured tasks will help children to develop initial movements in order to achieve high-quality outcomes.

Using Compositional Devices

Once children create movement material, they can develop and add composition devices. These make dances more interesting and exciting to perform and watch because dances are transient and require special moments that help the dancers and the audience engage with the meaning or dance idea. Three of the simplest devices that children can learn to use are **climax, contrast** and **repetition**. In the early stages of dance, children will learn about these by participating in dances that you have structured for them. Through appropriate task setting, they will be able to apply them to their own compositions.

Table 2.3   Composition Skills Used in Two Dance Ideas

	Bubbles (4- to 6-year-olds). See Toys unit on web resource ▶	Spring cleaning (6- to 8-year-olds)
Stimulus	Pot of bubbles with wand	Dusters, scrubbing brushes, squeegees, brooms, mops
Respond	Children watch and listen as teacher blows bubbles; they imagine what it would be like to be inside a bubble.	Children demonstrate how to use equipment; others describe actions and imitate without props.
Contribute	Create a word bank that describes shape, size, appearance, actions (e.g., round, grows, rises, drifts, wobbles, turns, clings, sinks, pops).	Create a list of actions to include in a spring-cleaning dance (e.g., dust, wipe, polish, scrub, sweep, mop, wash, gather, scoop).
Explore ideas	Explore the idea of *round*; talk to a friend and think of ways to show *round* in a dance.	Explore each action with a clear mime.
Create material	Action: Grow into a large rounded shape; rise, drift and sink. Space: Small to large; low–high–low. Dynamics: Slow, smooth and light. Relationship: On own.	Action: Mainly hand and arm gestures. Space: On spot. Dynamics: Strong and rhythmic. Relationships: Facing a partner.
Select material	Choose another action from the word bank to add (e.g., spin, wobble).	Choose 2 contrasting actions and practise these with partner.
Develop material	Dance with a partner to make the round shape; perform phrase as before.	Action: Add travel and turn or jump. Space: Repeat actions to each side. Dynamics: Use 2 speeds or vary the rhythm. Relationships: Introduce idea of opposites (up and down or side to side).
Include compositional devices	Add a climax: The bubble pops silently as it lands; show contrast in size, shape, speed and action.	Decide how many times to repeat the phrase of actions and show contrast in use of space (opposites).
Shape and structure	Ask the children how to combine phrases to make a class dance or structure it for them (i.e., all perform solo phrase—no pop—then the partner sequence). End with a pop.	Pairs combine to make groups of 4. Learn and combine phrases to make a group dance that must have clear beginning, middle and end, contrast and climax.

Vocabulary and Terminology

Using appropriate words to talk about dance is a two-way process that will result in a richer spoken and movement vocabulary. Conversely, active learning through the medium of dance will enrich children's written and spoken words. Dance in education, unlike ballet, does not have a specific terminology; it does, however, have a vocabulary that children and adults can use and apply accurately to describe, analyse, interpret and evaluate dance. This vocabulary includes words relating to these aspects:

- Actions (verbs)
- Dynamics (adverbs and adjectives)
- Space
- Relationships
- Expressive and sensory qualities: how feelings and meanings are perceived

- Formal qualities relating to the form, structure and composition devices
- Aspects of production: costume, accompaniment, set and lighting
- Physical and expressive skills

The youngest children are able to talk about their own and others' dances using a simple vocabulary. They can describe what they have done or can see, state preferences and give opinions. Following are teaching strategies for developing vocabulary and appreciation skills:

- Clear learning outcomes, emphasising key words, shared with the children
- Success criteria that children agree on
- Key words and a dance vocabulary on display

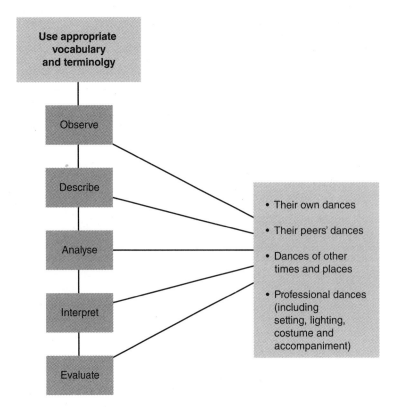

Figure 2.4 Appreciation skills and knowledge.

- Opportunities to draw, talk and write about dance
- Opportunities to reflect on own dances and observe others, including professional works
- Effective questioning to develop thinking and language

Critical Appreciation Skills

Critical appreciation is the ability to observe, describe, analyse, interpret and evaluate performance and composition. These skills, to a certain extent, are hierarchical in that observation and description are the simplest and evaluation is a high-order thinking skill (see table 2.4).

The following is an example of how a child might respond to Gene Kelly's solo from the film *Singin' in the Rain* (1952). It demonstrates the levels of critical appreciation that could apply equally to children talking about their own or others' short dances (see table 2.5). Having watched the film extract and considered the various elements, the children could apply some of the ideas to their own dances. See *Rain Again* and *Umbrellas* units of work on the web resource.

Peer and Self-Evaluation

Evaluating their own and each other's achievements will improve children's performance and composition. Both the processes and the outcomes can be evaluated—this represents good practice in teaching and learning and is a fundamental assessment for learning strategy (see chapter 7). Other assessment for learning strategies, such as clear learning outcomes and success criteria that are shared with the children, will also support the critical appreciation process. Encourage children to comment positively and constructively on what they have done or can see. They could evaluate using "two ticks and a wish"

Table 2.4   Critical Appreciation Skills

Observe	Watch actively
Describe	Set in words what is seen or heard
Analyse	Examine closely; identify elements
Interpret	Link movement to meaning; explain the meaning
Evaluate	Assess effectiveness or impact

(i.e., two things that are successful and one thing that they think could be improved or would like to see more of); or they could use "tickled pink and green for growth" (i.e., something that meets the success criteria, or pink, and something that could be improved, or green).

Feedback, whether from children or adults, should always be constructive. The ability to receive and respond positively to feedback, and to act on it, is equally important. Children need time to take on board suggestions for improvement and apply them in the lesson. Stating opinions or preferences should always be supported by reasons, such as "I liked Mason's clown dance because he pulled funny faces." In a key stage 1 dance based on *Singin' in the Rain*, the children could create a short movement phrase using three types of step for travelling around, over and through the puddles. They could select and order the steps and decide on a pathway. The self-evaluation checklist would be as follows:

- Do I have three different types of steps?
- Does my phrase have a clear order with a beginning, middle and end?
- Does my phrase have a clear pathway?

These success criteria could also apply when evaluating each other's sequences.

In a key stage 2 dance lesson based on creating a winning street dance, each group of critical friends could evaluate another group's dance focusing on the following criteria:

- Performance: good timing, good energy, teamwork
- Composition: different dance relationships, good beginning and end and a surprise at some point

In dance lessons, teachers rely a great deal on peer feedback and evaluation. Very few schools have mirrors that can provide effective feedback (but can also be distracting); however, iPads and video and digital cameras provide invaluable tools for self-evaluation.

Appreciation of Dance in Various Contexts

Dance appreciation has been made easier by the availability of dance on film and the opportunities to attend live performances. Photographs can also provide a good starting point for engaging with dance in various contexts. By the time they are 11 years old, children should appreciate that dance comes in many forms and that people all over the world dance for different reasons. Many children who watch TV dance shows such as *Strictly Come Dancing* talk knowledgeably about how well the celebrities perform, and they can also distinguish between styles such as a tango and a jive. Dances from other times and places used as a starting point for creative work will develop an awareness of dance styles and contexts. The process of critical appreciation described earlier can apply when viewing such dances.

Table 2.5 Critical Appreciation of *Singin' in the Rain*

Skill	Question	Sample answer
Describe	What did you see when you watched the clip from *Singin' in the Rain*?	A man sang and danced in the street. It was raining and he had an umbrella.
Analyse	What actions did he use?	He mostly used steps and he jumped on and off the pavement. He also spun around and opened his arms wide.
	How did he use the space?	He travelled along the pavement and danced in a circle in the road.
	How did he move?	He was relaxed but bouncy. He was sometimes fast. His energy matched the music, and he made different rhythms with his feet.
	Whom did he dance with?	He danced on his own, but he used an umbrella as a partner and met a policeman at the end of the dance.
Interpret	What do all these things tell us about the man and why he was dancing in the rain?	He was really happy and he didn't care about the weather. He enjoyed getting wet.
Evaluate	Which parts of the dance did you think were best, and why?	I liked it when his movements got bigger and he danced in the road and splashed in the puddles because it went with the music. I also liked the different ways he used the umbrella. It was interesting, and I wondered what he would do with it next.

Dance in Production

Professional works (dances created for audiences) on DVD are a valuable resource for teaching and learning dance in secondary education; they are an integral part of many courses in Britain. Younger children can be introduced to a range of suitable professional works, particularly if they can relate their own dances to them. Primary-age children have studied the works of well-known visual artists and composers as part of a balanced curriculum but professional dance works were not available until recently. It is important that children see models of good practice and also that they understand that dance is a profession that has many related roles. An excerpt of a professional work provides plenty of material for teaching and learning (see chapter 9).

The basic features of dances are as follows:

- Number, gender and role of dancers
- Subject matter or idea
- Movement material: actions, space, dynamics, relationships
- Starting point (or stimulus)
- Style
- Form and structure
- Choreographic devices
- Set (including props, scenery, backdrop, furniture)
- Lighting
- Costume (including footwear, accessories, masks, makeup)
- Accompaniment
- Use of camera (if appropriate)

The choreographer's selection and use of these features help the audience to understand the meaning of the dance by providing information about mood, time, place and character. How each relates to the other, the movement and the dancers helps communicate the intention of the choreographer. The many roles of those who contribute to a dance production, as seen in a theatre programme or on film credits, can be of interest to children and young people. Knowledge of these roles aids appreciation of dance as an industry as well as appreciation of the work itself. Such roles include the following:

- Choreographer
- Dancers
- Composer
- Musicians
- Sound engineer
- Costume designer
- Wardrobe assistants
- Set designer
- Lighting designer
- Stage manager
- Hair and makeup artists

Integrated Approach to Performance, Composition and Appreciation

The three processes of doing, making and reviewing dance are mutually dependent. Whilst a lesson objective might be to focus more on one aspect than the others, it is virtually impossible to exclude any of the three. For instance, in a lesson where the children are practising a dance before performing to an audience, the teacher will focus on performance skills. However, some peer evaluation (appreciation) will improve performance, and reference to the structure of the dance or composition devices such as climax and contrast (composition) will enrich the performance. Effective teaching will provide opportunities for children to experience the roles of performer, choreographer and audience member and to switch from one to the other seamlessly.

Table 2.6 shows the first lesson from a key stage 2 unit of work based on street dance (see *A Winning Dance* unit of work on the web resource). It outlines the learning activities

---

Task

To develop dance appreciation with colleagues or children, find three or four photographs or video clips (go to www.bbc.co.uk/learningzone/clips/dance) showing people dancing for different reasons. Use the following headings to encourage description, analysis and interpretation. Colleagues or children can then discuss and compare dances even if they are unfamiliar with them.

- Who is dancing?
- Where are they dancing?
- Why are they dancing?
- When were they dancing?
- What actions are they performing?
- What are they wearing?
- How are they dancing (movement quality, relationships)?

Table 2.6   A Winning Dance

Learning activity	Skill set
Watch excerpt. In groups, identify what makes a winning dance.	Appreciating
Sort ideas into performance and composition skills.	Appreciating
Warm up in street dance style focusing on mobility, rhythm and strength.	Performing
Learn a short phrase of basic moves. Practise and refine with a partner to achieve good timing.	Performing
Pairs observe pairs and feedback on performance skills: energy and timing.	Performing and appreciating
Practise in groups of 4 to achieve good unison.	Performing
Work in pairs again to develop initial phrase in terms of space, dynamics and relationships.	Composing
Pairs combine again in groups of 4 to share ideas.	Composing
Each group selects and combines ideas to create an interesting group phrase that has variety and contrast.	Composing
Groups observe each other and give feedback on success of timing, energy, teamwork, variety and contrast.	Performing and appreciating

experienced by the children and highlights the role they take in each activity. The lesson uses an extract from the film *Street Dance* (2010) as a stimulus. The learning outcome for the lesson is to perform and develop a section of a group dance in street dance style, focusing on good teamwork.

Summary

Dance has had curriculum status since the start of the 20th century, and the established model for dance in education today (with dual emphasis on process and product) has developed from the health-focused set folk dances in 1909 and movement enjoyed for its own sake in the 1950s. Rudolf Laban's analysis of movement and space underpins much of what is taught today, and the processes of performance, composition and appreciation provide the artistic tools. A strong focus on the composition (dance-making) process when planning and teaching primary dance is essential because this cannot happen without performance and appreciation.

Ingredients of Dance

Design is striking, rhythm is rousing and dynamics is a subtle colouring.

Doris Humphrey (1959, p. 104).

This chapter looks at the elements of dance and constructs a vocabulary around them. Practical examples and tasks illustrate each of the four ingredients: action, dynamics (including rhythm), space and relationships (see figure 3.1). These, combined with the processes of performing, composing and appreciating, form the recipes from which dances are created. Every movement has an action, dynamic and spatial content and, when performed with someone else, a dance relationship. An example is two children running (action) lightly (dynamic) along a zigzag pathway (space), one behind the other (relationship).

Actions
What the body does

Ingredients

Dynamics
How the body moves

Space
Where the body moves

Relationships
How we dance
with others

Figure 3.1   Ingredients of dance.

Actions
(What the Body Does)

The actions that can be used as dance material are categorised as follows:

- Travelling
- Jumping
- Turning
- Gesture
- Stillness

A small number of actions do not fit neatly into one category, such as falling (mainly a whole-body gesture with some weight transfer) and rolling and cartwheeling (travelling and turning). Individual units of work and lessons may focus on specific types or groups of actions. For example, a unit on traditional folk dance might focus on stepping and turning, but an effective scheme of work will encourage children to explore, develop and use a full range of actions. As children develop, they are able to perform a range of more complex combinations of actions such as travelling combined with gesture or turning combined with jumping. Figure 3.2 provides a word bank for each type of action.

> **Task**
> ___
>
> To create a chance dance, prepare a set of cards, each with an action written on it. Each child selects two or three cards and explores the actions before creating a movement phrase. These can be shared and combined with a partner or in a group to make longer phrases or short dances. Younger children could roll large dice (with a different action depicted on each side) to decide the order of actions.

Travelling is the transfer of weight in order to move across space by using the feet or other body parts (e.g., stepping, sliding, crawling or slithering). Variation in stepping is achieved by changing the size, height, speed and strength of steps; using different parts of the foot; or gesturing with the free leg whilst stepping.

> **Task**
> ___
>
> With the children, make a list of words to use instead of *walk*. Ask the children to make footprints in imaginary snow or sand. Encourage them to use different sizes of steps and various pathways, directions and parts of the feet to leave interesting tracks.

Jumping (or **elevation**) occurs when the body leaves and returns to the floor using the feet and legs as springs. A jump could be as small as a hop or as large as a leap. Different types of jumps are achieved by using either foot or both feet for taking off and landing:

- One foot to same (hop)
- One foot to the other (leap)
- Both feet to both feet (spring)
- One foot to both (hopscotch)
- Both feet to one (hopscotch)

Variations are also achieved through size, height, length, direction, body shape, power and leg gestures whilst in the air.

Travel		**Turn**		**Gesture**	
walk	run	whirl	twirl	punch	expand
creep	dash	rotate	pivot	contract	stretch
dart	limp	spin	pirouette	reach	flop
stagger	shuffle	spiral	revolve	quiver	collapse
glide	swoop	whip		nod	shake
tiptoe	scurry			point	shrug
scuttle	waddle	**Stillness**		wave	twist
plod	march	pause	hold	crouch	wiggle
scramble	trot	stop	freeze	clap	stamp
stride	strut	balance	halt	jerk	
slide	crawl	settle	suspend		
slither	saunter	wait	hesitate		
amble	slide	hover			
		Jump			
		spring	bound		
		leap	pounce		
		prance	skip		
		gallop	buck		
		hop	vault		

Figure 3.2 Action word banks.

Task

Ask the children to show various ways of jumping over, around, in and through imaginary puddles. Older children could draw up a list of types of animal jumps and explore and combine those to make movement phrases.

Turning involves rotation around an axis. Variation is achieved by body shape, the size of rotation (quarter, half, three-quarter turns), use of one or both feet, level and speed. Turns require an impetus, such as a step, and could also be initiated by a body part, such as an arm.

Task

Children choose two turning actions from the word bank and talk about what makes each different. Ask the children to imagine they are champion figure skaters gliding across the ice and to find three types of turns to perform. Encourage variety in body shape, speed, use of feet and level.

A star jump performed with good leg extension.

Gesture is the movement of part of the body or the whole body that does not involve weight bearing or transfer of weight. These include axial movements such as bending, stretching and twisting. Gestures are used in dance to enrich the expressive content and help communicate the meaning, but they could also be abstract. Gestures are used in some dance styles such as Bharatanatyam (Indian dance) and classical ballet to tell the story using a recognised symbolic vocabulary.

Task

To develop your understanding as a teacher, draw up a list of gestures (one for each key part of the body and some that are performed by the whole body).

Task

Ask the children to make up hand gestures for the following: water, wind, bird, fish, flower, moon, stars and sun. Use these to tell a story without words.

Stillness is the ability to control equilibrium or to stop a movement. Variation in balances can be achieved through different body shapes, levels, sizes of base and use of body parts and surfaces to form the base.

Task

Ask the children to choose two stillness words from the word bank and explain the difference. As part of the warm-up, play musical statues, providing progressive challenge by moving and stopping on the spot, then add turning, travelling and jumping.

Actions might be performed by specific parts of the body in **isolation** or **coordination.** For instance, in a robot dance, the children could isolate different body parts, moving them one at a time, then coordinate arms and legs to travel. Body parts could also lead the action. For instance, the arm could open out and lead the dancer into a turn. Some dances might emphasise

A moment of balance.

Gentle or explosive dynamic movement.

certain body parts, such as hand gestures in some Indian dance styles or use of hands and feet in South African gumboot dancing. The movement of body parts might be **successive**, as in a rippling arm movement, or **simultaneous**, as in a star jump. It is important for children to develop a good awareness of their bodies and how each part can move. In the early years, dances based on puppets, robots and mini-beasts will encourage children to explore the movement of limbs and joints in isolation and coordination.

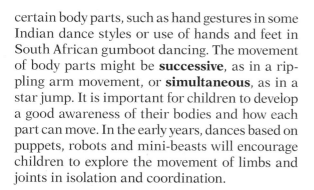

Task

For a key stage 1 warm-up, ask the children which parts of the body they can shake (or circle) to warm up. Create a shaky or circling warm-up. This task reinforces the names of joints and body parts and awareness of the range of motion in different joints.

Dynamics
(How the Body Moves)

Dynamic qualities provide the colour and texture of movement. Laban's analysis resulted in four motion factors or elements of weight, space, time and flow. The elements commonly referred to today are force, speed and **continuity** (or flow). Each can be considered as a scale with two extremes and many grades in between, as shown in figure 3.3.

Every action has shades of energy, speed and continuity. For instance, a punching action is strong, fast and abrupt, whereas a floating action is light, slow and continuous. The selection, combination and blend of dynamics provide the

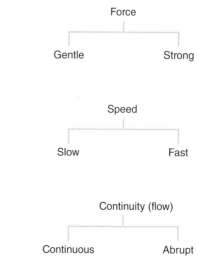

Figure 3.3 Elements of dynamics.

Task

Imagine these actions:

- Floating on air
- Wading through deep water
- Balancing on a high wire
- Free-falling
- Surfing a giant wave
- Sticking like glue
- Running across hot sand
- Freezing and melting
- Turning to jelly

Reflect on which dynamic qualities would be appropriate for each action. Ask children to do the same and then to select and explore three of these actions. Can a partner guess which they are performing?

clapping, patting and clicking). Rhythmic movement is a distinctive feature of some dance styles, such as jazz and street dance. Using a variety of dance accompaniment, particularly from diverse cultures, across the primary age range will provide different rhythmic experiences for the children (see chapter 9).

Task

With the children, look at Gene Kelly's solo in *Singin' in the Rain*. Can they pick out three different rhythms that he makes with his feet and clap them? Ask the children to use the rhythm of their first name and surname, clap it and then create an action phrase. They can combine these with partners or in small groups to make longer action phrases.

expressive content of dance. A range of rich and interesting descriptive words and imagery when talking about dynamics will enhance children's understanding. Figure 3.4 provides a word bank for dynamics.

Rhythm is an aspect of dynamics in that it comprises the elements of energy and speed. Rhythm might be natural, as in the rise and fall of breathing or the pumping of the heart. Rhythm can also be found in everyday actions such as walking. Occupational actions that have rhythm could form the content of dances such as in a harvest dance that comprises sowing and planting imaginary seeds and cutting and gathering imaginary corn. Rhythm (where beats are grouped, **accented**, patterned and repeated) is also suggested or dictated by musical accompaniment or created by body percussion (tapping,

Tip: To spell RHYTHM, remember **r**hythm **h**elps **y**our **t**wo **h**ips **m**ove!

Space (Where the Body Moves)

This is the visual design of the dance. As well as providing visual interest, the way in which space is used can help communicate the meaning or the idea of the dance. Some aspects of space such

melting	explosive
crumpling	smooth
floppy	powerful
tense	delicate
mechanical	robotic
sharp	drifting
flowing	jerky
percussive	soft
bouncy	relaxed
strong	gentle
energetic	quick
slow	fluid
heavy	light

Figure 3.4 Word bank for dynamics.

Contrast in levels and body shape.

as shape and level are physically obvious; other aspects such as air patterns are imagined. It is a good idea to approach space as something that is dynamic and tangible and can be manipulated, disturbed, surrounded, penetrated and repelled. Aspects of space to consider in dance are shown in figure 3.5.

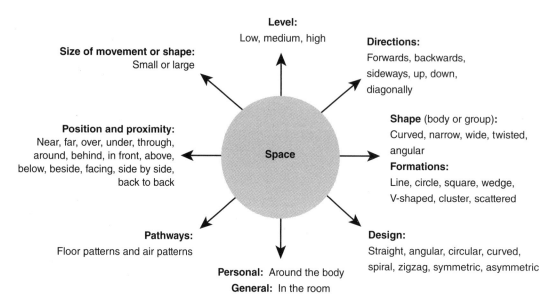

Figure 3.5 Aspects of space.

Relationships (How We Dance With Others)

Relationships describe the way in which dancers move with each other. They can be developed and varied in space and time and also through action. Dance relationships add visual interest and support the meaning or the dance idea.

Relationship devices, from copying to counterpoint (see figure 3.6), are set out in a progressive way in that copying another child or the teacher is the simplest dance relationship of all and counterpoint can be the most complex. Copying, **mirroring** (using opposite body parts) and leading and following (one behind the other) are skills that are introduced in the early years in warm-up activities and in action and singing games. Being the leader

Balance consisting of complementary shapes (parallel lines).

requires additional skills in that it takes responsibility and the ability to generate movement. Following requires good observation and kinaesthetic awareness. Meeting and parting is a spatial feature, forming part of the vocabulary

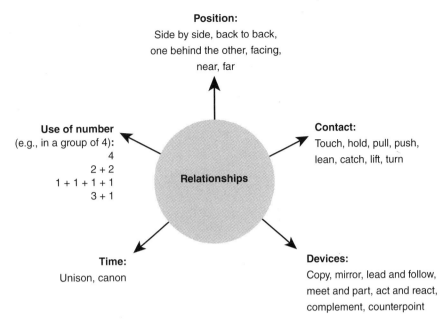

Figure 3.6 Aspects of relationships.

of **traditional** dances. It is also a feature that can be used as a **transition** in a class dance, such as when individual children join with a partner and then meet up to form groups. **Action and reaction** happens when one dancer moves and the other responds—like having a conversation in movement. It is a good way to explore contrast in shape, size and dynamics. **Complementary** shapes and actions occur when one dancer echoes another by creating a similar shape or action that is not exactly the same. For instance, one dancer might be standing tall with arms raised to create a Y shape; his or her partner might be kneeling in front with arms raised in a Y shape. The shapes are similar but different because of the levels used. **Counterpoint** occurs when two or more dancers perform different actions or phrases simultaneously that fit together. For instance in a dance about fireworks, three children start close together and travel apart and then jump and fall at the same time. Their travelling steps, jumps and falls might be different, but the relationship in time and space is clearly communicated.

Simple **relationships** in time are achieved when two or more dancers perform the same actions at the same time (**unison**) or the same actions but overlapping in time (**canon**). These are musical terms that dance shares.

Dance provides a safe context for developing the skill of contact, which requires trust, sensitivity and physical respect. It can be developed from an early age through simple partner and circle dances and can progress to confident weight taking and contact work required for dances like rock 'n' roll and the jitterbug, which can be performed by 10- and 11-year-olds. **Contact** refers to the use of touch, body parts in contact, sharing weight and taking weight. Many dances include opportunities to link body parts or shapes with those of a partner or in a group, and traditional folk dances encourage the use of a range of holds whilst travelling and turning with a partner or as a group. Activities that encourage children to create shapes that surround a partner or travel over, under and through each other's shapes will develop physical sensitivity.

Task

Ask the children to work in pairs and take it in turns to move over, under, around and through each other's shapes. This idea works well as an obstacle course travelling across the room (see Mission: Impossible in the scheme of work).

Sharing weight includes actions such as leaning, pulling (**countertension**) and pushing (**counterbalance**). These actions require body tension and the ability to give and take depending on a partner's size and strength. Taking weight occurs when a partner lifts the other or supports them in a jump and is suitable for older primary children. Taking weight requires a stable and wide base and both dancers to have good control and body awareness; it is also advisable to keep the momentum of the movement going. The supporter can create ledges, or surfaces that can take weight. The pelvic and shoulder regions are the strongest and safest for this. Children enjoy exploring lifts where they are back to back or standing side by side with arms linked and hips aligned. A simple assisted jump can be explored with partners facing each other, one with hands on the partner's shoulders and the supporter with hands on the partner's waist. The child being lifted must provide the impetus to jump. This simple jump can be developed in a number of ways; for instance, the supporter can turn as they lift and put their partner down in a different spot, or both children could face the same way and the child being lifted could perform a star jump.

Countertension provides good support.

Knowledge of the movement material that dance comprises will enable you to plan effective dance lessons and units of work, provide high-quality experiences and hold high expectations of what children can achieve in dance. Table 3.1 demonstrates how the ingredients of dance work together to support skills and knowledge in dance.

> ### Task
>
> Children sit with partners on the floor and explore ways of leaning, pulling and pushing against each other whilst staying on the spot.

Summary

Every movement has action and dynamic and spatial content (and when performed with others there is a relationship). A secure understanding of the ingredients of dance and of what movement material comprises is fundamental to teaching dance. Actions, dynamics, space and relationships form the movement vocabulary for performance and composition, and the ability to discern and describe these is vital to the appreciation process.

Table 3.1   Combining the Ingredients

Mission: Impossible	
Context: A high-energy dance based on secret agents that includes individual, partner and group work. Lesson 1 focuses on exploring and selecting appropriate actions and developing a partner sequence.	
Actions	Create a word bank of suitable actions (e.g., crawl, dodge, duck, dive, slide, freeze, swerve, skid, creep, crouch, jump, zigzag, leap, edge, balance, pause). Explore some whilst travelling around the room and add moments of stillness.
Dynamics	Vary the speed and strength of the actions. Which will be the quickest, slowest, strongest, lightest?
Space	Explore all 3 levels and use different directions. Include imaginary obstacles to travel over, under, around or through. Make a clear pathway in the room.
Relationships	Lead and follow a partner on this mission and copy actions exactly. Select 3 actions and create a unison partner sequence with a clear beginning, middle and end and a clear floor pattern. Add or include canon and contact.

From Ideas to Dances

This chapter provides guidance and support in structuring a dance experience. Also presented are teaching and learning strategies, types and styles of dance and a variety of stimuli. The chapter ends with a brief look at choreographic principles and approaches. This knowledge will help you work more effectively with children to achieve interesting and successful dance outcomes.

Planning the Dance Experience

Ideas for dance are likely to come from two sources. The first is a curriculum topic, theme or focus for a particular term or half term. The second source is the children's needs and interests. You might have noticed, for instance, that children would benefit from developing better spatial awareness, movement memory or cooperation skills. For an experienced dance teacher, these considerations go hand in hand and come naturally. The scheme of work on the web resource provides support if you're a less experienced teacher, and the overview of the units of work provides an outline for each. The themes and ideas have clear links to the curriculum, enabling children to learn both in and through dance. Table 4.1 provides an overview of the planning process.

The next step is to identify the **learning outcomes** in the form of skills and knowledge at the appropriate level. These are based on expectations for the primary years, which are covered in detail in chapter 7. Each expectation can be expanded and broken down into learning outcomes for medium- and short-term planning. It is a good idea to have one performance, one composition and one appreciation outcome in each lesson. The expectations can be summarised as follows:

Performing

- Move with control, coordination, extension and fluency.
- Copy, repeat and remember actions, phrases and dances.
- Perform a range of actions.
- Use a variety of dynamics.
- Use space confidently.
- Use expression to communicate meaning.
- Show musicality.
- Understand and demonstrate safe practice.
- Perform with confidence, concentration, focus and projection to a range of audiences.
- Perform dances in a range of styles.

Composing

- Respond imaginatively to a range of stimuli.
- Explore and experiment with movement ideas.
- Develop movement using actions, dynamics, space and relationships.
- Work with others to create and structure dances.
- Use simple compositional devices.
- Use accompaniment sensitively.
- Create dances in different styles.

Appreciating

- Describe dances using appropriate vocabulary.
- Interpret meaning and intention.
- Evaluate own and others' dances.
- Identify areas of improvement in own and peers' performance and composition.
- Show awareness of different dance styles and contexts.

The next decision regards the **type** of dance, which often relates to the stimulus and theme. It might be narrative (interpreting a story), abstract (a dance inspired by shapes and patterns), comic (a dance inspired by cartoon characters), traditional (a dance exploring folk dance figures and formations) or **lyrical** (a dance inspired by a piece of music). Or it might relate to a specific dance style such as street dance. Some thought must be given to types of dance so that children will experience a broad and balanced range in the school year and key stage. These, together

Table 4.1 Planning the Dance Experience

Idea	What is the curricular theme or focus, and what learning needs and interests could I address?
Learning outcomes	What performance, composition and appreciation skills and knowledge do I want the pupils to achieve?
Type of dance	What kind of dance will it be (e.g., narrative, abstract, comic)?
Stimulus	What will I use to introduce the idea?
	Will it motivate learners?
	Will it inspire movement?
Starting point	What are the key words?
	How and when will I introduce the stimulus?
	What will initiate movement?
Accompaniment	What kind of music is best?
	Could I use silence or percussion?
	Get to know it thoroughly.
Movement content	Select movements relevant to the idea.
Structure	Plan in terms of body, action, dynamics, space and relationships.
	Plan tasks that allow pupils to explore, select and develop actions and create sequences of movement.
	Structure the learning by planning a series of tasks.
	Have an idea of the overall shape the dance will take over a series of lessons.
	Be prepared to modify the structure as you proceed.
	Children could help decide the final outcome.

with styles of dance, are explored in more detail later in this chapter. The next step is to select an appropriate **stimulus (or stimuli)** that will inspire and engage the pupils and provide movement ideas. Key words or a word bank can provide starting points for generating movement material, and you will then need to consider what sort of **accompaniment** would help achieve the mood, communicate the meaning of the dance and provide elements of structure for the dance. Children will develop rhythmic and dynamic awareness if they experience a range of types of accompaniment and styles of music. Chapter 9 explores accompaniment in detail.

The next step is to decide the movement content. Exploring the stimulus should help you to identify and map out the appropriate actions, dynamics, space and relationships and then select the movement ideas

that will translate into tasks and ultimately form sections of the dance. You should have an idea of a dance structure. This may be dictated by the theme or type of dance or by the accompaniment. A flexible approach allows the structure to be modified as the dance progresses, and it is always

Using a painting as a stimulus.

good practice to give the children ownership of the dance by taking their structural ideas and suggestions. Listening to the accompaniment might provide some points of reference. It could have repeated **phrases** or sections such as verses and choruses, contrasting sections, climaxes and a clear beginning and end.

Stimuli for Dance

A stimulus is something that inspires or triggers a response. Artists, whatever their art form, draw inspiration from the world around them and produce work in response. In the primary school environment, teachers use a range of visual, auditory and kinaesthetic resources to engage and motivate children in learning across the

Task

Find a stimulus from each category in table 4.2 and reflect on how each might inspire dance.

curriculum. Many of these are likely to provide appropriate stimuli for dance. The senses of sight, sound and touch help you to engage with stimuli and young children. Those with little dance experience and those with specific learning needs will respond better if they see or touch the stimulus, which might be a story book, object or video clip. Suitable dance stimuli provide triggers that will prompt actions, shapes, feelings or designs.

Table 4.2   Examples of Stimuli and Their Features

Type of stimulus	Examples	Features that support dance ideas	Dance example in scheme of work
Auditory (words)	Words, phrases, instructions, recipes, poems, stories, text	Meaning, movement words, rhythm, repetition, structure, sounds, phrasing, narrative	The Loner uses words, phrases and the theme of a poem.
Auditory (sounds)	Styles and types of music (e.g., classical, pop, traditional, electronic), sound effects, percussion, body percussion, spoken word	Style, culture, form, structure, tempo, mood, meaning, lyrics, rhythm, pattern	Rock 'n' Roll uses the structure, style and rhythm of a song.
Visual	Photos, paintings, sculptures, mobiles, environmental art, cartoons, collages, graffiti, everyday objects, films, video extracts	Character, place, representation, symbolism, abstraction, colour, shape, line, texture, pattern, form	Umbrellas is inspired by Renoir's painting of a busy scene with umbrellas and the shapes and features of umbrellas.
Kinaesthetic	Movement of an object, animal or person; dances or movement phrases; people at work, rest or play; everyday activities	Actions, relationships, pathways, dynamic qualities, mood, atmosphere	The Snowball deconstructs and reconstructs a traditional folk dance.
Natural	Landscapes, locations, weather, the elements, geographical features, climate, outer space, forces, electricity, chemical reactions, growth, the animal world	Shape, form, movement, pattern, effects on living things	Rain Again! responds to rain, in its many forms, exploring the idea of puddles, rainfall, thunder and lightning.
Ideas and concepts	Historical events, topical events, important issues, moods, emotions, random ideas	Human behaviour, actions, movement patterns, feelings, moods, interaction, relationships, groupings, formations	Mission Impossible is inspired by the actions of secret agents.
Props and accessories	Streamers, ribbons, hoops, hats, gloves, boots	Size, shape, how it moves, how you move with it, how it affects the dancer, mood, meaning	In Tiddalik streamers are used to encourage and enhance fluid movements for the water section.

Examples of stimuli and their features can be seen in table 4.2. Stimuli (or starting points) for dance can be grouped as follows:

- **Auditory**, as in words or music
- **Visual**, as in pictures or objects
- **Kinaesthetic** (sensing the movement) as in other dances
- Natural, as in science and nature
- Ideas and concepts
- **Props** and **accessories**, as in things people wear for dance or that people dance with

Planning From a Stimulus

The process of planning dance from a stimulus is similar to the composition process described in chapter 2. By following this, you will be able to plan for structured tasks that will enable the children to experience the composition process for themselves and create their own short pieces of dance or complete dances. Figure 4.1 shows how similar these two processes are.

The following is an example of this planning process using the painting *Our Town* by L.S. Lowry as a stimulus for a key stage 2 dance (*Our Town*).

1. Brainstorm with selected words underlined: going and stopping, indoors and outdoors, different ways of walking, buildings (factories and homes), windows, doors, lines, repetition, activity and purpose, different people (age and character), pairs, conversations, crowds, bleak, cold, grey, colourless, and so on.

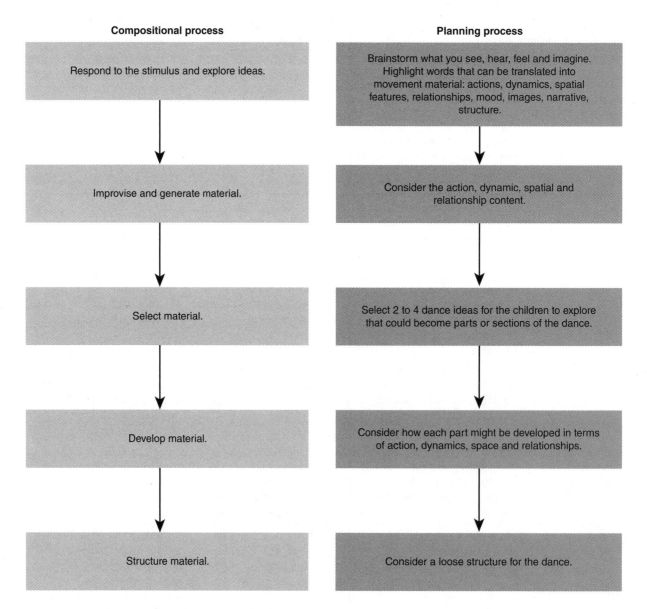

Compositional process

- Respond to the stimulus and explore ideas.
- Improvise and generate material.
- Select material.
- Develop material.
- Structure material.

Planning process

- Brainstorm what you see, hear, feel and imagine. Highlight words that can be translated into movement material: actions, dynamics, spatial features, relationships, mood, images, narrative, structure.
- Consider the action, dynamic, spatial and relationship content.
- Select 2 to 4 dance ideas for the children to explore that could become parts or sections of the dance.
- Consider how each part might be developed in terms of action, dynamics, space and relationships.
- Consider a loose structure for the dance.

Figure 4.1 Comparison of the composition and dance planning processes.

2. Selected dance ideas: steps and step patterns, busy street scene, different characters, factory work.

3. Movement material for each idea:
   - Steps and step patterns: ways of stepping to show mood, character and age (action)
   - Working in pairs in unison (relationships)
   - Busy street: directions of travel and pathways (space)
   - Characters: expression, posture and gesture (action)
   - Group unison (relationship)
   - Factory work: rhythmic working actions (action and dynamics)
   - Group unison, action and reaction (relationships)

4. A possible structure:
   a. Busy street: painting comes to life; pairs are still and ready to travel across the canvas with their step patterns.
   b. Dancers group together and perform a simple travelling sequence in unison as a class.
   c. Characters meet up in groups to perform a gesture pattern (on the spot) as selected type (children, teenagers, mums, old folks).
   d. Groups repeat unison travelling sequence to take them to work.
   e. Groups perform factory work sequence.
   f. Unison travelling sequence to take them out of work and into a space with partner.
   g. Create the painting again (still positions).

This is one example of a structure in rondo form. The children could suggest how to structure the dance once they have worked on and completed various sections. The unison travelling sequence provides a useful transition between the sections and could take the dancers to different places in the space if necessary. There are lots of opportunities in this dance unit for developing compositional skills: the children explore steps and gestures and create movement patterns of each, and they develop sequences of

working actions. Performance skills are required for learning the unison travelling phrase, perfecting unison work in pairs and groups and remembering the movement material. They will develop their expressive skills to show character in facial expression, posture, gesture and travelling. Appreciation skills are needed for evaluating their own and each other's movement ideas and outcomes and making improvements. They could also view an excerpt of *A Simple Man* (Lynne et al. 2010) on DVD. This ballet was choreographed by Gillian Lynne in response to the paintings of L.S. Lowry, and it shows some great characterisation and street scenes.

Structuring the Learning

Tasks must be set that enable the children to explore, select and develop actions, phrases and short dances and also develop their performance, composition and appreciation skills. These tasks might include individual, partner and group work depending on the age and experience of the children. Generally speaking, it is good practice to do the following:

- Set tasks that allow for experimentation.
- Make teaching points from observations.
- Provide opportunities for the children to select material.
- Set tasks that enable children to create phrases and short dances.
- Encourage the development of material by repeating, varying, extending and changing body parts, actions, dynamics, space and relationships.

Exploring space and responding individually.

- Allow time to improve, practice and perfect.
- Encourage self-evaluation and peer evaluation throughout, not just at the end of the lesson.

Remember that as the teacher, you are the facilitator and the children are the choreographers. Also, remember to have *fun*!

Planning for Progression

A successful **scheme of work** in dance will

- reflect the ethos of the school,
- belong to those who deliver it,
- be regularly reviewed and updated,
- be flexible so that it meets teachers' and children's needs,
- provide challenge and high expectation,
- provide progression and continuity and
- be enjoyable.

The scheme of work on the web resource included with this book is based on the following principles:

- High-quality outcomes (see chapter 1): the skills and knowledge children should acquire by the end of the year or key stage
- Progression and continuity
- Amount of time per year, term, week and lesson
- Opportunities to perform, compose and appreciate
- A range of stimuli to reflect children's needs and interests
- Cross-curricular links, topics and themes
- A range of styles and cultural contexts
- Different types of dance
- A range of accompaniment
- Assessment opportunities
- Alternative ideas for stimuli and accompaniment, where appropriate

This scheme is not intended to be prescriptive. It is envisaged that schools and teachers will select the units that meet the needs of their children and the curriculum in order to provide a broad and balanced dance experience. Another intention is for teachers to use the scheme to develop their confidence to plan and deliver their own dance ideas.

For each phase (reception, key stage 1, lower key stage 2 and upper key stage 2) there are a number of dance ideas, each introducing a new type or style of dance inspired by a different stimulus. These are **units of work** (medium-term plan) that set out what is to be covered across a number of lessons or weeks, most likely four to six. A unit of work should include the following:

- Clear learning outcomes relating to skills, understanding of performance, composition and appreciation
- Details of the dance content covered: actions, dynamics, space and relationships
- Resources required (including accompaniment, stimuli, DVDs of professional works)
- Cross-curricular links, shared stimuli and common concepts
- Teaching and learning activities
- Assessment strategies

Older children will be able to sustain, develop and build on a dance idea over a number of lessons or weeks, whereas the youngest children require a range and variety of dance experiences that could be linked by a theme, such as in the Toys and What a Week! units.

The scheme of work contains units of dance, each of which lists appropriate tasks or activities but not individual lessons. You can therefore decide what is to be taught in each lesson to meet the children's needs and suit the time available.

Each dance lesson (short-term plan) should focus on elements of unit of work, such as these:

- Clear learning outcomes
- The dance content to be covered
- Key vocabulary
- Resources required
- Teaching and learning activities
- Assessment opportunities

The following model lesson structure (see table 4.3) is a key stage 1 lesson based on Spider-Man. The learning outcome is to create and perform a high-energy dance that explores Spider-Man images and actions. In this first lesson, the children explore a range of appropriate actions and create a partner sequence. The lesson provides a balance of discussion and observation (10 minutes) and dancing (25 minutes). Lessons in key stage 2 will ideally last longer (45 minutes) with up to 10 minutes to explore the dance idea and up to 15 minutes for the main task.

Table 4.3   Structure of a Model Lesson

Time	Task type	Activity
5 mins	Share lesson outcomes and success criteria. Recap previous learning if appropriate.	Introduce dance idea. Children look at pictures of Spider-Man and create a word bank of actions (e.g., spin, jump, swing, shoot (web), crouch, walk up and down walls and on ceilings, freeze, balance, leap).
5 mins	Warm up.	Teacher leads a warm-up sequence introducing some of the actions: hands walking up an imaginary wall, reaching, dropping into a crouch, swinging from thread to thread across the space.
5 mins	Introduce and explore idea.	Children explore balancing on 1, 2 and 3 body parts; travelling on 3 planes ("walls", floor and "ceiling"); spinning webs and shooting threads from wrists.
10 mins	Main task: Select, develop and refine dance material.	In pairs, children choose 3 actions from the word bank to make a short unison phrase that is performed with energy. They develop the phrase to include simple relationships in space and time. They practise and refine their phrase.
5 mins	Review achievements and talk about next steps.	Each pair works with another pair to evaluate and give feedback on achievements. You and the children share ideas for what might happen next.
3-5 mins	Cool down.	Slow and gentle stretches, lying on the floor.

Teaching and Learning Strategies

Teaching is a complex activity. Your personality and style of teaching have as much impact on the children's responses as the resources that have been selected and the dance idea itself. There has been an increased focus in education on teaching styles and preferred learning styles and also on the difference between boys' and girls' learning styles. Whatever the teaching or learning style, it is important to employ and experience a range of strategies in order to be effective teachers and learners. Teaching strategies are the methods, ideas, devices and approaches that facilitate learning.

Exploring Spider-Man images and actions.

These strategies (which help you set the tasks) should be fit for purpose in that they help the learners meet the desired outcomes. In the United States Mosston and Ashworth (1986) categorised a spectrum of teaching styles to assist PE teachers (see table 4.4). They range from teacher directed at one end of the spectrum to student initiated at the other.

Awareness of children's preferred learning styles will help you remove some of the barriers to learning because children do not all learn in the same way. Research on learning styles such as **VAK** (visual, auditory, kinaesthetic), Gardner's (1993) **multiple intelligences** (visual-spatial, linguistic, kinaesthetic, logical-mathematical, musical, interpersonal, intrapersonal, naturalistic) and Gregorc's (1986) **thinking styles** (abstract sequential, concrete sequential, abstract sequential) has had a significant impact on classroom practice in recent years. As far as VAK strategies

Table 4.4 Teaching and Learning Strategies Used Frequently in Dance

Strategy	Definition	Dance example
Command	Teacher directs or instructs.	Teaching and learning a warm-up sequence
Demonstration or modelling	Teacher or learners demonstrate what is required.	Watching a good example of a phrase created by others in the class
Divergent or problem solving	Teacher sets a task and invites learners to discover solutions.	Working as a group to combine and link ideas
Games	Movement games with rules that encourage different responses.	Follow-the-leader step patterns
Guided discovery	Learners are led to experience movements and concepts decided by the teacher.	Jumping over, around and in imaginary puddles to learn about the types of jumps
Inclusion	Learners choose and work at their own level.	Choosing to link 2, 3 or 4 actions to make a phrase
Occasional instruction	Teacher sets a task and as learners progress, teacher adds to the task.	While children travel around the room, ask them to change direction and then level.
Practice	Learners are given time to rehearse and improve aspects of their work.	Practising a sequence to improve expressive qualities of focus and projection
Questioning	Teachers or learners pose various questions to develop thinking, check understanding or assess.	Children responding to teacher's questions about the aspects of production of a dance they watch on DVD
Recall	Verbally or physically return to previous learning.	Going over the sequences created in the previous lesson or earlier in the lesson
Reciprocal teaching	Learners work in pairs or groups collaboratively or as teacher and learners.	Watching a partner perform and giving feedback
Selected response	Learners select material from improvisation and exploration tasks.	Teacher setting 3 tasks exploring aspects of winter (e.g., a snowball fight, footprints in the snow, freezing and melting) and children selecting ideas from these to create their own group dance
Specific limitation	Teacher imposes restrictions in order to encourage problem solving.	Children travelling across the space using 3 levels
Whole–part–whole	Teacher breaks down the whole into parts and puts them together again.	Teach a sequence, break it down into separate actions, then build it up again.

are concerned, dance holds a privileged position in that the learning style is predominantly kinaesthetic. Dance therefore engages children who learn best when involved in physical activity and who might lose concentration and interest if they are sitting for lengths of time. However, an effective dance lesson includes strategies that address a range of preferred learning styles:

- Using a visual stimulus (visual)
- Encouraging discussion and designing word banks (auditory and linguistic)
- Exploring movement ideas (kinaesthetic and abstract random)
- Setting problem-solving tasks (problem solving and concrete random)
- Providing musical accompaniment (musical)

- Providing opportunities to create dances with others (interpersonal)
- Asking children to evaluate their own performance and composition (intrapersonal)

The scheme of work on the web resource contains a variety of dance ideas that ensure a broad and balanced dance experience for each age and stage of the primary phase.

Types of Dance

Dances fall into broad categories, and the types that are most appropriate for primary children are commonly known as abstract, comic, dramatic and pure. Dances often contain elements of more than one type. Several factors influence the type of dance:

- Type of stimulus (starting point)
- Subject matter or theme and how it is treated
- The way in which the movement material is created and developed
- Type of movement used (e.g., literal, symbolic or abstract)
- The relationship with the accompaniment
- The dance outcome (i.e., how we want the audience to feel)

Abstract dance explores themes and ideas in a non-representational way whilst keeping an essence of the idea that is still recognisable. A dance based on electricity, for example, would be abstract.

Comic dance usually includes **mimetic** gestures, character, exaggeration and an element of surprise. Timing and quirkiness also add humour. A dance based on cartoon characters would be a comic dance.

Dramatic dance might be narrative, where a story unfolds, or it could explore an aspect of the human condition such as an issue, mood or emotion in a non-narrative way. A dance exploring playground relationships and loneliness would be dramatic.

Pure dance is concerned with movement itself and does not set out to communicate any particular meaning or to express an idea other than this. A chance dance using chance to select and sequence action content would be a pure dance.

 The units of work on the web resource contain a variety of the types of dance that children should experience. For instance, the units for years 1 and 2 include an abstract dance inspired by paintings, a dance based on the Bollywood style and a dramatic dance based on an Aboriginal story.

Styles of Dance

Dancing is a way of expressing something about ourselves and the values and beliefs of the groups, communities and countries to which we belong. Most dances share the same ingredients of actions, dynamics, space and relationships; but the way in which they are selected, combined and performed gives them different flavours, which we recognise as styles. The wide range of styles in Britain today is continually evolving and blending to create new styles. Families of styles (known as **genres**) are umbrella terms such as contemporary, ballet, jazz, ballroom, urban and folk dance. Each genre has a range of styles that share similar features. For example, **contemporary** dance includes styles influenced by Martha Graham and Merce Cunningham, contact improvisation and release. The African and South Asian dance genres include many styles that share common features. Every dance comprises technical features and a vocabulary of movement that are the essence of the style. The following elements and the way in which each is performed tell us a lot about the style:

- Stance: Upright or relaxed? Wide or narrow? How is the body aligned?
- Centre and spine: Contracted or extended? Does it tip or tilt? Used a little or a lot?
- Body parts: Which are emphasised? Isolated or coordinated?
- Initiation: Where in the body does the movement originate?
- Actions: What are the predominant actions—steps, jumps, turns, gestures or stillness?
- Gestures: Mimetic or abstract? Precise? Natural? Recognisable patterns?
- Floor work: Movements to, on and from the floor?
- Body design: Shapes? Angular or curved?
- Dynamic qualities: Use of speed, flow, strength, energy and weight?
- Rhythmic qualities: Which body parts are involved? Even? Metric? Accented?
- Relationships: How do dancers dance together? Contact? Roles? Partnering?
- Attitude: Facial expression? Overall impression?

Awareness of the essential features of a style will help you to get inside and teach it effectively and creatively. For instance, you can deconstruct and develop the features of the tango as a group or class dance by exploring the following:

- Upright stance
- Straight back, with occasional tips and tilts
- Sharp head movements and leg kicks
- Gliding across the floor on one level
- Linear pathways with changes of direction
- Smooth and sudden combinations of dynamics
- Strong rhythmic interest and relationship with the music
- Close contact with others
- Serious and dramatic attitude

Dance both defines and transcends cultures, and this makes it a valuable teaching and learning tool. Learning about dances from different cultures enriches children's movement vocabulary and challenges their technical, expressive and creative skills, as well as enriching their knowledge of the world of dance. Dances from other cultures often have a strong visual and musical identity that engages and stimulates both boys and girls, and children are naturally curious about less familiar and different ways of moving. Dances from other cultures also provide a good trigger for cross-curricular learning (see chapter 8); for instance, learning about Bollywood dance could enhance learning in music, geography and religious education and develop coordination, movement memory, spatial awareness and teamwork.

As a teacher, you do not have to be an expert in every dance style. But to capture the essence and share it with the children, you will need a good understanding of the ingredients of dance; how to develop the skills of performing, composing and appreciating; and how to use resources effectively. You will also need to be able to identify the features of a particular style. You need to respect the style and culture from which each dance comes and be informed of the context and relate it to the lives of the children who are learning it. For example, the **Bhangra** harvest dance has similarities to the English Morris dance: Both were danced by men and originate from rural communities. They are also energetic and athletic.

The most appropriate resources that inform teaching and learning are the dances themselves, ideally demonstrated by an expert (who could be a parent or friend of the school, a member of the community or a professional artist). After the event, effective teachers will find ways to develop and build on the initial input:

- Including the dance as part of a narrative using a traditional story from the culture
- Encouraging the children to use the new vocabulary creatively by developing the action and dynamic, spatial and relationship content
- Creating a display that includes photos of the children dancing and their evaluations of the experience
- Cascading the experience (children as teachers) to other classes
- Sharing the work in assembly

If it is not possible to learn a dance from an expert, the next best resources are films and video clips, which are easily accessed on the Internet. Careful observation and analysis by the children will enable them to draw up a word bank for exploration. The appropriate music can provide both stimulus and accompaniment by establishing mood, atmosphere, dynamics and rhythm. Traditional costumes and props will provide and enhance movement ideas and

artefacts (i.e., objects) from the culture being studied can also stimulate movement ideas. For instance, a length of printed fabric from Africa could provide ideas for body and group shapes, floor patterns, motifs and repetition. Stories from other cultures often provide very good starting points for dance ideas; several examples are in the scheme of work on the web resource, such as Handa's Hen (from Africa) for reception and Pan Gu (from China) for years 3 and 4.

The most popular cultural dance styles in primary schools today come from African and South Asian traditions.

> ## Task
>
> Work with colleagues or children to create a simple dance for pairs or groups based on traditional British folk dance that comprises travelling, turning, meeting and parting. Perform it to music from a different time or place. How does the music affect the movement?

African Dance

Each of Africa's 54 countries has its own style and variety of dances, so it would be unwise to describe African dance as if it were one style. Generally speaking, African dance and music are coexistent; singing and vocal responses often form an important element. The drums determine the rhythm, structure and movements; the style of playing and instruments are particular to a region. The education pack and DVD *Coming Home* (National Resource Centre for Dance 1988) include a range of African dances performed by the pan-African dance company Adzido. African dances vary in purpose and origin and include the following:

- Dances for celebrating initiation, war and harvest
- Social dances, usually for younger people
- Welcome dances
- Dances for fortune and good luck
- Dances to prepare for events such as a battle
- Dances that are specific to settings, such as the gumboot dance, which originated in the gold and diamond mines of Southern Africa
- Dances that share religion, history and stories

Following are common features of African dances:

- Flexed feet
- Low centre of gravity
- Bent knees and elbows
- Mimetic gestures
- Relaxed posture
- Rhythmic movements of shoulders, chest and pelvis
- Body parts used in isolation and coordination

Here is a simple celebration dance in African style (it is also a warm-up on the web resource):

- Stand in a circle with feet slightly apart, knees slightly bent and hands on hips.
- Move shoulders alternately forwards towards the centre of the circle, leaning forwards slightly.
- Keep shoulders still and move hips from side to side with the body more upright.
- Wave both arms high above the head from side to side, allowing hips to move from side to side.
- Shake both hands low to one side of the knees and then the other.
- Repeat each movement several times, then use 8 counts for each to create a repeatable pattern.
- Stamp and clap on the spot (slower tempo than the previous actions).

These actions can be developed by turning to face a partner and stamping and clapping to travel around each other or by stamping and clapping into a space to meet up in groups of three or four and repeating the main sequence. The children could then add their own celebration actions to develop and extend the sequence.

South Asian Dance

This term embraces classical Indian folk, popular and contemporary dance styles. There are seven main styles of classical Indian dance and those most commonly seen in Britain are Bharatanatyam, Kathak and Kathakali. Each style has its own characteristics, but they all share three elements:

1. Natya (drama)
2. Nritya (mime and movement)
3. Nritta (stylised poses and footwork patterns)

Common features are stylised facial expressions, complex rhythmic patterns (usually emphasised by the feet) and hand gestures known as mudras or hastas. A maxim in classical Indian dance is "where the hand goes, the eyes should follow". The way in which the eyes follow the leading hand draws the audience in and provides a good starting point for creative exploration of this genre.

Bharatanatyam originated in the temples of Southern India. It has driving percussive energy, geometric spatial design of the body and precise footwork.

Kathak originated in the story-telling traditions of North India and developed through the Hindu courts. It includes complex footwork, fast spins and sudden, still poses.

Kathakali originated in Southwest India. It is vigorous and dramatic with elements of martial arts. Kathakali depicts characters from Hindu myths and legends using highly stylised mime, makeup and costumes. It is traditionally danced by men.

Here is the process for creating a simple dance in classical Indian style:

- Make a collection of photographs of Indian dance poses.
- Look at these carefully and analyse the positions: body shape, design, hands, feet, focus.
- Each child chooses three positions to copy and links them to make a smooth sequence (linking actions are led by the hands with the eyes following).
- Children work in pairs to teach each other their sequences and combine ideas to make one longer unison sequence.
- This can be developed by including repetition, rhythmic patterns, steps and turns.
- Develop the relationships by including canon and mirroring.

Task

Ask the children to sit facing a partner and explore hand and arm gestures. (Use gentle Indian music as an accompaniment.) They then select three to link into a phrase and perform as if in a mirror. These can be developed by doing the following:

- Stand up and make the actions larger (space).
- Add actions such as travel and turn (actions).
- Introduce variety in speed (dynamics).
- Include repetition (other).
- Perform side by side (relationships).

Bollywood is a more recent style of South Asian dance that originates from the Hindu film industry but is more often associated with the entire South Asian film culture. It combines music, dance and theatre and usually involves the hero, heroine and large chorus. The dances often provide fantastic or dream-like escapism. The style includes elements of Bharatanatyam, Kathak and folk dance styles, often blended with Western styles such as street dance.

Choreographic Knowledge for the Teacher

This section introduces features of choreography that will enable you to build successful dances with children. Good subject knowledge leads to high expectations. When you model choreographic devices and principles to the children, they will be able to do it for themselves. Following are choreographic principles that are appropriate to use with primary children:

- Motif and development
- Repetition
- Contrast
- Highlights and climax
- Relationships

Motif and Development

Motifs are the key to creating and developing dance material. They are phrases of movement that embody the style and the content of the dance; they have action and dynamic and spatial content and can therefore be developed in many ways. As well as being a structural element, motifs help the audience to recognise and understand the meaning or dance idea. Figure 4.2 gives an overview of how motifs can be developed.

Repetition

Like music, dance relies on an element of repetition to reinforce an idea and help the audience remember significant moments. Repetition also helps communicate the meaning. It contributes to the structure of the dance, such as with a chorus or an ending that echoes the beginning and provides reference points for the dancer. Practical examples can be seen in the Calabash Children and Rock 'n' Roll units of work. Overuse of repetition can lead to boring and predictable outcomes.

Contrast

This is achieved by adding something new or by changing an aspect significantly, such as the

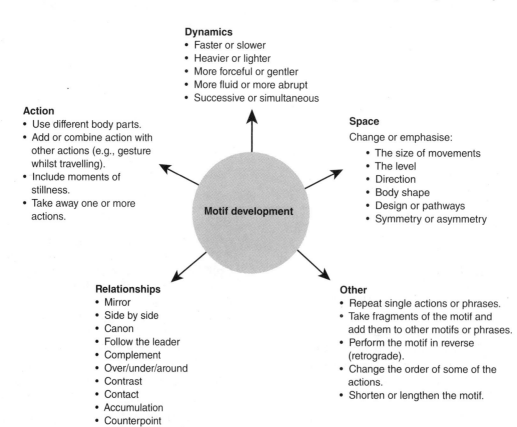

Dynamics
- Faster or slower
- Heavier or lighter
- More forceful or gentler
- More fluid or more abrupt
- Successive or simultaneous

Action
- Use different body parts.
- Add or combine action with other actions (e.g., gesture whilst travelling).
- Include moments of stillness.
- Take away one or more actions.

Motif development

Space
Change or emphasise:
- The size of movements
- The level
- Direction
- Body shape
- Design or pathways
- Symmetry or asymmetry

Relationships
- Mirror
- Side by side
- Canon
- Follow the leader
- Complement
- Over/under/around
- Contrast
- Contact
- Accumulation
- Counterpoint

Other
- Repeat single actions or phrases.
- Take fragments of the motif and add them to other motifs or phrases.
- Perform the motif in reverse (retrograde).
- Change the order of some of the actions.
- Shorten or lengthen the motif.

Figure 4.2 Motif development.

dynamic qualities or the size of the movement. An example can be seen in Our Town when the children stop travelling with their step patterns and perform gestural patterns on the spot. The choice of accompaniment is important because it can provide suitable dynamic contrast. A good example can be seen in the film *Singin' in the Rain* where the size of the movements in the dance to the title song matches the orchestration of the music.

Climax achieved through unison, stillness and focus.

Highlights and Climax

These are the significant moments that the audience will remember after the dance has finished and that communicate the meaning or dance idea effectively. Again, the *Singin' in the Rain* solo provides a good example of climax and highlights. **Climaxes** can be achieved in a number of ways:

- Unison
- Increasing or decreasing the number of dancers
- Speeding up or slowing down the action
- Stillness
- Formations or group shapes
- Making movements larger

Relationships

As well as being key ingredients, relationships are a **choreographic device** in that they contribute to the structure of the dance. They add interest and variety and can enhance and emphasise the meaning or dance idea. Relationships are mainly achieved through varying time, space or use of number (see table 4.5).

Odd numbers in dances (such as trios and quintets) create asymmetry and more opportunities for dance relationships and dramatic effect. Even numbers (duos and quartets) can create a more balanced and formal effect.

Structure

The structure (also called **form**) is the way in which the content of the dance is ordered and shaped. In simple terms, structure is the begin-

> **Task**
>
> Teachers, watch the solo dance from *Singin' in the Rain* once through and then close your eyes and recall three moments that you can remember clearly. Which are highlights and which might be a climax?

ning, middle and end of the dance. Dance, like music, happens over time and has therefore borrowed musical terms to describe dance forms:

- **Binary** is a dance in two parts where the second section provides contrast but is linked by theme.
- **Ternary** is a dance in three sections with the middle section providing the contrast.
- **Rondo** has a chorus section that remains the same with each section between being different to the one before.
- **Narrative** is where a story line unfolds a section at a time.

Whether it is a group or a whole-class dance, the beginning of a dance will set the scene and mood and get the audience's attention. The end of the dance is what stays in the audience's memory. American choreographer Doris Humphrey (1959, p. 159) provided dancers with the following tips:

All dances are too long. . . . a good ending is forty per cent of the dance. . . . don't leave the ending to the end.

Table 4.5 Relationships Suitable for Use With Primary-Age Children

Unison	When all dancers perform the same action
Mirror image	It can be used to achieve symmetry where half the dancers move in one direction and the other half move in the other direction.
Complementary	Actions or shapes are similar but not identical.
Question and answer	A conversation in movement between two dancers or two groups. One performs and the other responds with a unison, contrasting or complementary action.
Accumulation	A sequence of movements is built up as more dancers join in until they are all dancing in unison. It can also be used in reverse.
Counterpoint	Dancers perform individual but different phrases at the same time.
Numerical variation	The way in which the number of dancers is used adds interest and can enhance the mood and meaning. For example, four dancers might enter the space one at a time (1 + 1 + 1 + 1); perform a sequence in unison; then split into two pairs to perform duos (2 + 2). Three could then perform in unison, with the fourth dancer staying still (3 + 1); and finish with a sequence performed in canon (1 + 1 + 2).

Beginnings and endings should reflect and communicate the dance idea and be fit for purpose. Consider the following:

- Whether all dancers will be on stage at the start and finish
- Exits and entrances
- Where in the space the dancers will start and finish
- Starting and finishing positions

Choreographic Approaches

Two approaches that are effective for use in primary schools are collage and chance. **Collage** is a way of piecing together different sections or ideas where the central theme is the unifying factor and there is no story line. For instance, the Umbrellas dance, inspired by Renoir's painting, comprises different sections: the busy crowd, a key unison motif based on umbrella action words, a duo developing the same words and a group section exploring umbrella shapes. These sections can be repeated and ordered to suit the accompaniment. **Chance** is an approach in which the movement material is determined using a random method such as flash cards or the throwing of a die to decide the next action, dynamic or spatial feature. Chance works well when there is a substantial word bank from which to draw ideas. Dice with clear sides for inserting words or shapes can be used with the youngest pupils. In Tiddalik, the children are given random animal action words to create their silly dance sequences—this encourages them to focus on the way animals move rather than being the animals.

Summary

This chapter, together with the scheme of work in the web resource, will support you in your short-, medium- and long-term planning. The dance planning process is similar to the compositional process, and it is important that you understand choreographic principles and devices. However, remember that the children should be the choreographers and that you, the teacher, are the enabler. Understanding and using appropriate teaching and learning strategies will facilitate this.

Warming Up, Cooling Down and Safe Practice

This chapter sets out the reasons for warming up and cooling down for dance and explains what happens to the body during these activities. The chapter also gives guidance on effective warm-ups and cool-downs and provides ideas, with practical examples, for structuring and organising suitable activities that can be developed over time. The final section provides a common-sense approach to safe practice in dance that will be of particular interest to visiting dance teachers and schools wishing to review their policies.

Warming Up

An effective warm-up sets the right tone and establishes expectations of what will follow in the dance lesson. It engages and energises the children and prepares them for dance physiologically and mentally. Effective warm-ups also promote the principles of safe practice. Following are essential physiological objectives of warming up:

- Prepare the joints for work.
- Engage the cardiorespiratory system by increasing body temperature and blood flow to muscles to make them more elastic.
- Prepare neuromuscular response patterns (i.e., increase the speed of messages from the brain to parts of the body).
- Prevent strain or injury.

This physiological activity will lead to improved performance. The technical skills required for effective performance (alignment, balance, control, coordination, core stability, extension, flexibility, mobility, posture, stamina and strength) are described in some detail in the performance section of chapter 2. Table 5.1 suggests tasks for developing each skill, many of which could be included in warm-up sequences.

Here are other benefits of warming up:

- Improve focus and concentration.
- Develop rhythmic phrasing.

- Create an opportunity to introduce a new dance style.
- Create an opportunity to introduce the content of the main body of the lesson or provide a contrasting activity.
- Improve movement memory.
- Develop performance skills (physical and expressive).
- Develop social skills.
- Develop spatial awareness.

For very young children, warming up is not really a physical necessity, but a focused warm-up will develop and enhance the children's understanding of how their bodies work, their vocabulary of actions and dynamics, their spatial awareness and their awareness of self and others. A safe and effective warm-up gradually raises the body temperature; increases circulation, breathing and energy; lubricates the joints; and works the main muscle groups. Children should understand why they are warming up and what these desired outcomes will be. Cognitive skills such as counting, remembering, sequencing, and thinking ahead will also be employed. The resulting improved focus and concentration required by an effective warm-up means that the children are less likely to have accidents and injuries.

A warm-up should take the joints and limbs through a full range of motion, increase the heart rate and prepare for the movement patterns to come. It is best to use short phrases that are simple and repetitive with actions that are steady and rhythmic. The recommended order is mobility followed by pulse raising and then stretching and, if required, strength work. Strength work is not entirely necessary in the primary phase, although older children, especially boys, enjoy the challenge, and all children will benefit from developing core stability. Strengthening should occur only at the end of a warm-up when the body is warm and **supple**. If the dance space is cold, it is important to take longer to warm up and also to gradually increase the intensity.

Table 5.1 Tasks for Exploring and Improving Physical and Technical Skills

Principle	Task
Alignment	• Stand with feet hip-width apart. Roll the chin towards the chest and continue to roll, curving the spine and bending the knees forward (over the toes). Fingers touch the floor. Reverse and unroll to stand tall. • Raise arms to the sides, shoulders down. Wiggle fingers until you can see them whilst looking straight ahead. This is good alignment.
Balance	• Balance on one foot and explore what happens when moving the free leg and both arms around to create various shapes and lines. Be aware of muscular tension needed for keeping movements smooth and holding positions. Imagine threads joining the hands and feet to each other. • Stand tall and rise on the balls of the feet. Focus on a still object ahead. Close eyes. What happens?
Control	• Musical statues: Walk, run, skip, hop and jump on the spot and around the space, freeze when the music stops.
Coordination	• Practise three hand gestures (e.g., clap, shake, punch) and combine each with a different foot action (e.g., march, jump, turn). • Sailors' hornpipe: Climb the rigging, look out to sea (right and left), skip on the spot, heave in the anchor. Repeat, performing faster and faster.
Core stability	• Sit or lie in a curled-up position. Breathe in and out slowly and smoothly; at the same time expand and contract the body from the centre. Make the movements larger each time to include limbs, but control from the centre. • See also sit-ups in Strength section.
Extension	• Reach up with straight arms and hands, shoulders down. Look at hands and let the energy flow from the centre along the arms and through the fingers—make arms even longer.
Flexibility	• To find turnout, stand with feet pointing forwards, tense muscles in legs and pelvic girdle, and rotate hips to turn out the legs and feet to about 45 degrees, keeping heels together. • Sit and draw up knees. Extend legs and torso forwards, keeping chest close to thighs. Repeat several times to increase flexibility.
Mobility	• Create warm-up sequences that include movements on the spot, travelling and changes in level (e.g., a roll). Encourage smooth transitions.
Posture	• When standing, imagine a golden thread through the body from the heels up through the spine and out of the top of the head; shoulders are down and neck is long. Always stand tall. • When sitting feel the sitting bones in contact with the floor. Sit up tall and remember the golden thread.
Stamina	• Walk, jog and skip on the spot or around the room along an imaginary pathway. Children stop when they think they have completed 1 minute. Use a stopwatch to tell them when 1 minute is up. Increase times until they can keep moving for 3 minutes.
Strength	• Stand with feet apart and imagine pulling down weights with both hands at the same time as bending the knees. Straighten the knees and push the weights to the ceiling. This exercise uses resistance in the body to strengthen the muscle groups. • Lie on back with knees bent and feet on the floor; roll up the head and spine until sitting up with a straight back with arms reaching forwards. Reverse to lie down.

Mobility involves warming up the synovial fluid and improving joint lubrication. Moving joints within their natural range will further enhance the range and the ability to absorb impact. An example of a mobilising exercise is circling the shoulders, wrists, hips and ankles.

Pulse raising involves increasing cardio-respiratory activity, which results in a faster pulse, faster breathing and raised body temperature. This encourages muscle elasticity, creates more energy and speedier muscle response and improves coordination. Pulse raising stimulates the muscle fibres used for power and strength and those used for balance and posture. Pulse raising does not necessarily require lots of jogging and jumping. Moving the hands and arms energetically above the heart, such as by repetitive clapping above the head or punching the air, will raise the pulse and warm some muscles; but moving the whole body (e.g., clapping and stepping) is the best approach.

Stretching muscles will maintain or increase flexibility. It is advisable to stretch the muscles that will be required for the range of motion required in the lesson. For the youngest children, simple whole-body stretches prepare for the learning that follows. **Dynamic stretches** are recommended when warming up. These entail moving the muscles and joints through their full range in a slow, controlled manner as part of continuous movement. An example of dynamic stretching is tracing large circles with the hands in front of and around the body on different planes.

Strengthening requires a common-sense approach because it is more appropriate for older primary children and best introduced as part of or towards the end of a warm-up.

A good warm-up engages and energises the body.

Boys in particular enjoy the challenge of strength work in exercises such as walking the hands along the floor into a plank position and lowering the body to the floor (as in a press-up) or reaching up or forward with alternate hands whilst in a plank position or bent-knee sit-ups. Repetitive steps and jumps also strengthen the body, but there is a health warning with these, as with some other exercises:

- Young children's bones are soft at the ends and therefore more susceptible to injury. So avoid activities that put bones and joints under excessive strain, such as repetitive jumping, especially on a hard floor without appropriate footwear.
- Children are less efficient than adults at performing short bursts of high-intensity activities. Avoid an excessive number of high-intensity activities, and space them out with adequate recovery periods.
- Discourage fast arm circling and uncontrolled swinging actions. These can lead to strains and small tears. All exercises should be performed with control.
- Avoid ballistic (bouncing) stretches. These can cause tiny tears, stiffness or soreness, and they have little physical benefit.
- Avoid head circling or snapping the head back because this can put strain on the vertebrae in the neck (atlas and axis). Instead, mobilise the neck gently by looking from side to side, tilting the head towards the shoulder and performing half circles (looking to the side, down, down, then other side).
- Avoid straight-leg stretches and straight-leg sit-ups because they put unnecessary strain on the lower back. Always keep the knees soft when standing and reaching towards the floor, and keep them bent when performing sit-ups.

A successful warm-up can last for several sessions and be revised from time to time. It should be fit for purpose and should be appropriate for the ages and abilities of the children. Generally speaking, three minutes is adequate for the very youngest children, increasing to six or seven minutes for 10- and 11-year-olds. The warm-up might be a general all-purpose activity to mobilise, raise the pulse rate and stretch, or it might introduce a specific theme, concept or style. It might even introduce a section of the dance that will follow later. The warm-up for The Calabash Children in the scheme of work becomes the celebration dance in this unit. Examples of other warm-up activities are on the web resource. Following are types of warm-ups:

- Themed: Circle body parts, tracing circles in space and travelling along a circular pathway.
- Top to toe: Mobilise the joints, starting with the shoulders (these should always be released before the head and neck), and then work down through the body.
- Sequenced: Develop a sequence of three or four types of action that can be repeated and varied, for instance, individually, with a partner and in a small group.
- Style: Introduce a specific style such as African dance by emphasising a low centre of gravity and soft knees, isolating shoulders and hips, moving rhythmically and coordinating gestures with steps.

- Socialising: Encourage children to relate to others, such as by meeting and greeting each other (waving, shaking hands, hugging) as they travel around the room.
- Games: Follow the leader or Fast Forward and Rewind (see web resource) where children follow instructions for travelling at different speeds and in different directions.

Having decided on the type of warm-up that is fit for purpose, select a lively, rhythmic piece of music that will engage the children. The music should be at an appropriate speed, and it might also provide repetition and sequence and therefore help structure the activity. Begin gently on the spot with a mobilising activity before raising the pulse by enlarging actions or adding steps and coordinating actions. Finish with simple whole-body stretches for younger children or more specific stretches for older children. Have three or four actions in mind that can form a sequence (see Mix and Match). Here is an example of a simple key stage 1 warm-up:

- Tap knees twice and then shoulders once and reach high (4 counts in all). Repeat several times, then extend by tapping feet, knees, and shoulders and reach high (4 counts).
- Shake hands high to low (floor), bending knees, then go back up to high taking 8 counts for 8 shakes. Repeat several times.
- March on the spot lifting knees and swinging arms. Keep in time with the music.
- Jog on the spot in time with the music. This is not the same as running; it requires strength and control and engages all of the joints and muscles in the feet and legs.

Once the children can perform each action well, form a longer phrase by taking 16 counts for each section and then reduce to 8 counts (but maintain the movement quality). You can develop this phrase by marching or jogging to a new space before repeating the taps and shakes. To end the warm-up, slow down the tapping section so that it becomes a slow-motion curling and stretching movement.

Organisation in Space

Warming up also provides an opportunity to develop and practise spatial awareness. Following are choices for arranging the children in the space:

- Start with children near you or in a space of their own.
- Have them start by sitting or standing.
- Arrange them in a circle.
- Have them stand in a line behind you or in shorter lines ready to follow the leader.
- Pair each child with a partner or arrange them in a small group.

Once routines are established, vary the use of space and explore options. For the youngest children, start with them sitting close to you (but without touching each other). For an older, unfamiliar class, begin standing in a circle, which provides equality and ensures that everyone can be seen. Both of these strategies provide the option to move individual children around so that everyone is able to learn effectively. An example for each of these strategies is provided in the Cold Day and Circle, Pair, Group warm-ups in the web resource.

Young children close to the teacher.

Progression

It is possible for a warm-up to develop and progress in a few minutes or from lesson to lesson. You can achieve this by developing, adding and combining actions and by developing or changing spatial features or relationships. Simple progression is achieved in the Cold Day Warm-Up by progressing from sitting to standing and then travelling and in the key stage 2 Circle–Partner–Group warm-up by starting in a circle, spacing out, relating to a partner and then performing in a group. Progression from lesson to lesson can be achieved in the following ways:

- Adding a bit more to the sequence each week
- Working in pairs or groups so children can add their own sections
- Changing spatial arrangements (e.g., facing different directions)

Ultimately the oldest children should be able to create their own effective warm-up sequences with a partner or in a small group. This is one of the successful outcomes of daily physical activity such as Wake and Shake in primary schools. Many teachers report that learning and memorising exercise sequences have developed children's movement memories, improved their physical skills and developed their knowledge of healthy living. Such sequences provide suitable warm-up activities for dance. The Mix and Match Warm-Up provides examples for mobilising, pulse-raising, stretching and strength work. You can select and combine ideas from the first two or three to create a general warm-up sequence. Ideas from the strength section would be appropriate to include in a warm-up for 10- and 11-year-olds.

Inclusive Practice

Children develop at different rates and in different ways, so it is important to ensure that they can all access warm-up activities, particularly because this type of activity is likely to be directed by you more so than in other parts of the lesson. Whatever their skill level, all children will benefit from learning patterns of movement and repeating these over a few lessons (with developments from week to week) as well as more open-ended exploratory or games-based warm-up tasks. Clear demonstration and

Older children creating group warm-ups.

verbal instructions from you are a given, and children with learning difficulties may benefit from performing simple actions slowly before increasing the pace and complexity, such as by learning the steps before coordinating the arm actions. For children with physical disabilities, consider the range of motion that is available to them and suggest substituting one body part for another. For example, a child in a wheelchair could move alternate shoulders or hands up and down instead of marching on the spot. You can adapt instructions for children using walkers or chairs so that they are able to perform sideways movements instead of travelling sideways. Partner or adult support is always welcome, and some children with disabilities would benefit from having a zoned space to move in. For more information about enabling all children to succeed, see chapter 6.

Cooling Down

Cooling down allows the heart to return to its resting state and helps prevent stiffness or soreness by avoiding the build-up of the waste products, such as lactic acid, in the muscles as the result of exercise. Cooling down also prevents the pooling of blood in the muscles, which could cause dizziness due to the reduced blood supply to the brain. Primary dance lessons are usually based on a range of natural movements and include opportunities to create and appreciate each other's work, so it is unlikely that the children will be dancing for sustained lengths of time. However, a brief cool-down activity establishes good practice, refocuses the children and returns the body and mind to a state of rest. A cool-down should provide a relevant conclusion to the lesson in the following ways:

- Lowering the pulse to help the cardiovascular system slow down gradually
- Stretching to maintain and develop flexibility in the muscle groups used
- Encouraging good, deep breathing
- Remobilising the joints

As with warm-ups, cool-down activities should be fit for the purpose. Possible activities include the following:

- Walking in and out of the spaces and slowing down as the rate of breathing slows
- Mobilising joints such as circling the shoulders and rolling down and unrolling through the spine
- Static stretching (holding stretches for at least 10 seconds)
- Dynamic stretching, such as curling and stretching on the floor, lying on back (whole-body stretch) or with weight on hands and knees and moving hips back to sit on the heels (for arms and back)
- Specific stretches, such as lunges forwards for calves and hamstrings and sideways for adductors and inner-thigh muscles, or lacing fingers together by turning hands inside out to stretch upwards and tilt or twist from side to side for arms and back
- Taking a sequence or movement phrases learned in the lesson and performing in slow motion but larger (to encourage dynamic stretching)

The two- to three-minute cool-down should end with a few moments of stillness and relaxation. The children could think about what they have achieved in the lesson, how they have improved their skills and what they have enjoyed doing most.

Stillness and relaxation refocus the mind.

Safe Practice

First and foremost, you must be familiar with the health and safety policies of the school and the local authority; maintain updated knowledge of legal requirements; and keep in mind how children grow, develop and learn. Whatever the activity or environment, you should always assess and manage the risks of an activity and make your expectations clear to the children and any other adults. Chapter 6 explains how to achieve a positive ethos for learning and how to manage behaviour, space and learning.

Your Responsibilities as a Teacher

As a teacher of dance, you should do the following:

- Be appropriately qualified or experienced.
- Comply with the school's safe-guarding requirements.
- Understand how the body works (its potential and its limitations).
- Know and appreciate children as individuals with a range of physical abilities.
- Understand how children develop and be aware of the physical and hormonal changes that take place during puberty and how they can affect performance in dance.

- Focus on the quality of movement and performance skills rather than technical ability.
- Value creativity.
- Build on the children's individual strengths.
- Use the age-related expectations in chapter 7 to plan and provide appropriate tasks.

You are in a position of trust and have a duty of care to your pupils. In the event of an injury and alleged negligence, you will be judged against the standards of a reasonable professional. You are advised to be appropriately insured. If you are working on a freelance basis, you need to have personal public liability insurance. It is also advisable to belong to an appropriate professional association and to undertake relevant criminal record checks. You must follow the school protocol with regard to taking photographs or videos of children dancing and how these may be posted on the school website. A school camera should be used, not a personal one, for this purpose.

Children should learn to recognise and understand safe practice so that they can take responsibility for creating a safe dance environment. It is important to teach them the following:

- That regular physical activity requires a balanced diet and plenty of water
- The importance of presenting themselves safely and appropriately for dance
- How to warm up and cool down effectively and why these are important
- To respect their own and others' bodies
- To maintain a tidy and safe dance environment

Children will achieve well in a learning environment that is both physically and emotionally safe. The indicators of emotional safety are the same for any teaching and learning activity, but they are especially pertinent in dance where the concern is about physical expression and, sometimes, emotional content. Therefore, you need to ensure the following:

- Relationships should be respectful.
- Behaviour management should be fair and consistent.
- Imagery and language have to be positive.
- Dance has to be inclusive, promoting equality and diversity.
- Self-esteem and confidence have to be promoted.
- Creativity and the quality of movement should be valued.

What to Wear

You should model good practice by dressing appropriately for dance. In most schools the practice is for children to wear their PE kits (shorts and a T-shirt) and have bare feet for dance. Older children may feel more comfortable in leggings or track suit bottoms rather than shorts. It may not always be convenient or possible to change into different clothes, such as for a short exercise session or a dance rehearsal, in which case it is advisable to remove shoes and socks, ties and outer layers. In many primary schools the children get changed in the classroom. However, it is more appropriate for older primary children to change separately—the school or local authority policy will provide guidance. Hair should be tied back and jewellery and watches removed and stored safely. It is often the practice to tape over ear or nose studs, and it goes without saying that gum chewing by adults or children should never be permitted.

Dancing in bare feet should be the norm because it

- strengthens the feet and improves flexibility, control and stability;

Dancing in bare feet should be the norm.

- helps to ensure alignment and correct use of muscles;
- improves the quality of movement, including extension; and
- enables the full range of motion.

Plimsolls do not encourage good walking, running or dancing because the soles are usually flat. If footwear is to be worn, trainers are preferable because they provide better support for the feet. Children should never dance in socks or tights because they may cause children to slip. Children should not dance in bare feet if

- they have foot infections, verrucae or other conditions;
- they are engaged in high-impact work involving lots of steps and jumps, such as in Rock 'n' Roll; or
- the floor is slippery, dirty, hard, carpeted or in poor condition.

Environment

A suitable dance space will

- be warm (a minimum of 18 degrees), well lit and well ventilated;
- have a floor with some give in it and a clean, non-slip surface (a sprung wooden floor is ideal);
- have no obstacles that could cause injury;
- be large enough to accommodate the children dancing; and
- have doorways and fire exits clear from obstruction and well signed.

If the space is not appropriate, then the activity should be adapted:

- If it is cold, spend a longer time warming up and allow children to wear jumpers.
- If it is hot, keep activities short and change the focus more often to aid concentration and ensure children drink plenty of water.
- If the floor is hard, dirty or slippery, wear trainers and do not let the children work at floor level.
- If the space is small, let the children take it in turn to work and watch.
- If there are obstacles, point out the dangers and avoid working in those areas (obstacles could be fenced off with chairs or benches).

Using Resources Safely

To safeguard children physically and mentally, ensure that any material that is used in the dance lesson is appropriate and that it supports the dance idea and the intended outcome.

- Props: Using props in dance is similar to using small equipment in other PE activities. The props should be in good order and safe to use and children should be reminded to take care of the props, themselves and others. When introducing props allow one group at a time to explore moving with them and for the rest of the class to observe and feedback, especially if the props (for instance umbrellas) take up a significant amount of space.
- Music: Make sure the content and lyrics are suitable for the age group. Always listen to music in advance of using it and avoid music with a "parental guidance" label but instead look for "radio edit" versions.
- Dance material and content: Ensure that the style, subject matter and movement material is suitable for the children's age and stage of development (both physical and emotional). Children may be exposed to explicit and suggestive dance material on some TV channels and pop DVDs at home, which they might accept as normal. Ideas, resources, stimuli and movement material relating to the primary curriculum such as those on the web resource provide appropriate content and styles for primary age children.

Dance Lesson

Here are the minimum requirements:

- An adequate warm-up to prepare for the physical demands of the lesson
- Emphasis on correct technique for executing actions such as jumping, turning and weight taking
- Group sizes that are appropriate to age, stage and space
- Tasks that build progressively from simple to more complex
- Children who have control over their bodies and of their learning
- A cool-down to return to resting state

Contact Work

Dance provides an ideal context for sensitive physical contact (see chapter 3). Physical contact includes body parts in contact, the various holds required in traditional folk and social dances, sharing weight and taking weight. Children will be sensible about touching if they have plenty of opportunities to develop physical contact through a variety of types and styles of dance from an early age. Support and weight taking require a level of maturity and strength and are therefore more suited to children in upper key stage 2. Children should be able to control their own bodies and weight before progressing to supporting others. They also need a good degree of body awareness and muscular tension so that they can make themselves appear lighter when supported rather than feel like dead weights. Here are general safety requirements:

- For the supporter to have a wide base with both feet flat on the floor
- A strong grip—grip each other's wrists, not hands
- To use shoulder and hip girdles for supporting weight, because they are the strongest body regions
- For centres of gravity of both dancers to be close
- Confidence, trust and mutual agreement
- Opportunities to practise
- To move slowly into and out of lifts with control
- To keep the momentum going where possible

There are times when it is both necessary and appropriate for you as the teacher to make physical contact with children, such as when making corrections or demonstrating. You should make your intentions explicit and public by saying something such as the following: "Do you mind if I use you to demonstrate?" "Is it okay if I take hold of you here and here?" "I am going to put my hand on your back where I want you to straighten it." You should never find yourself alone with single children in dance or in any other context.

Injury Prevention and Management

Everyone using the dance space must take some responsibility for safety, and sharing the assessment of risks is part of the learning process. However, as the teacher, you are ultimately responsible for the safety of the children in your care. So it is important for you to do the following:

- Ensure that children are hydrated. Water should be available for children in dance

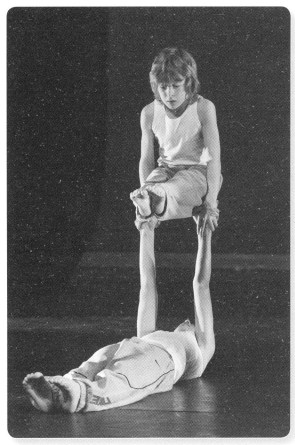

Weight-taking requires maturity and strength.

sessions (especially when it is hot) and during prolonged work such as rehearsals, festivals and concerts.
- Have up-to-date first aid training and know who the school first aider is.
- Know when to refer to a medical practitioner.
- Follow appropriate reporting procedures for accidents.
- Be prepared for minor injuries such as sprains and strains and know how to deal with these appropriately.

The most common dance injury is a sprain, which should be treated by following the RICED procedure:

- Rest: Stop dancing and sit down.
- Ice: Apply an ice pack (wrapped in a towel) for 10 minutes to reduce pain and swelling.
- Compress: Apply a firm bandage round the affected area to control the swelling.
- Elevate: Raise the injured limb.
- Diagnosis: Refer to a medical practitioner if unsure or concerned.

Summary

There is no doubt that an effective warm-up will engage even the most reluctant dancer who will then go on to enjoy the rest of the lesson. The warm-up will be effective only if it increases the heart rate and mobilises the joints. As the examples in this chapter and on the web resource demonstrate, it is important to provide variety in types of warm-up and to treat every task as a learning opportunity rather than a routine to get through in order to move to the main part of the lesson. You and the children have a responsibility to ensure that the learning environment in dance is physically and emotionally safe and one in which individuals can develop confidence and self-esteem and have their achievements valued and respected.

Managing the Learning

This chapter focuses on managing the children, their behaviour and the space in order to create the best conditions for learning. The suggested strategies will be of particular interest to dance teachers who are visitors to the school or who are not the children's regular teachers. This chapter also explores elements of inclusive practice, including how to make provision for children with physical disabilities or learning difficulties and talented and gifted children. The chapter ends by exploring gender issues in dance and suggesting strategies for engaging boys in dance and improving perceptions of boys who dance.

Establishing an Ethos

A little subject knowledge can go a long way in the dance lesson, but how do you create the right conditions for learning? The three aspects that might worry an inexperienced teacher of dance are also what make dance exciting. First, dance requires minimal resources (apart from space and, perhaps, accompaniment). Second, movement is the medium. Third, in a creative context the finished product is unknown or unexpected. In other words, children moving in a large space with very little equipment and few resources can be scary! So, how do you engage children? Here are some strategies:

- Brisk pace and structured tasks
- Variety of activities and group sizes
- Having children create their own dances and have ownership of the material
- Fun tasks that encourage problem solving
- A product to work towards, such as a finished dance to share with others

The tips that follow apply to all subjects, so considerations of how each applies to the dance context have been added.

Tips for Developing a Positive Ethos

1. Have high expectations, and set these at the start of the session. A visiting dance teacher might say, "I know I am not your normal teacher, but in this lesson I expect . . ."

2. Model the behaviour expected. Be polite and respectful; join in and have a go; wear the right clothes for dance; meet and greet the children as they arrive.

3. Establish routines: how they enter and leave the dance space, where to put belongings, where to sit for the start of the lesson.

4. Share expectations and be consistent. Agree on the rules for learning and behaviour, use consistent rewards and sanctions.

5. Praise and motivate to raise self-esteem and engage the children.

6. Build physical and emotional respect. Children should respect each other's bodies, ideas and achievements.

Join in and dress appropriately.

7. Provide enjoyable sessions. Use stimuli, content and accompaniment that the children can relate to.

8. Teach with humour, warmth and passion.

9. Use positive body language. Make eye contact, be relaxed and have an open posture.

10. Use the voice effectively. Manage, motivate and achieve the quality of movement by varying the pitch, tone and volume; know when and how to project your voice.

Managing Behaviour

Even with the best will in the world and all the elements for good learning conditions in place, there will be odd occasions when children's behaviour in dance is not exemplary, so it is important to have some strategies ready to pre-empt poor behaviour and to manage it appropriately. Good behaviour management is proactive rather than reactive. Poor behaviour in dance includes off-task chatting, not listening and not following instructions. Depending on the context and frequency, this behaviour could be unacceptable. Unacceptable behaviour includes pushing or tripping others and executing uncontrolled or dangerous movements. Lack of respect for others' work could also be considered unacceptable. At worst, poor behaviour diminishes the learning and enjoyment of others, affects safety, spoils relationships and destroys respect. It can also prevent you from teaching when you spend more time with a minority of children in the class.

Schools focus on positive behaviour management by praising and rewarding good behaviour rather than admonishing negative aspects. This is effective because, at heart, every child seeks adults' approval. Turning negatives into positives by using positive language is especially effective, for instance, saying, "I like the way that group is working together…" rather than "Your group is too noisy". Visiting dance teachers will require help in order to become familiar with schools' behaviour policies and the rewards and sanctions that apply to activities before, during and after the school day. It is also important to provide visiting teachers with information about the behavioural needs of the individuals in their care. The widely used four Rs have been increased to five (see table 6.1) to provide teachers and children with a clear framework for promoting behaviour for learning.

For managing poor behaviour in dance, follow the school's policy. You may also need to create a set of hierarchical consequences, such as these:

1. Have a warning and rule reminder.

2. Remove the child from partner or group and move him or her to a different partner or group.

3. Have the child sit out for 2 to 4 minutes until you or the child feels that the child is ready to join in again.

4. Report the behaviour to a senior member of staff.

5. Remove the child from the session (only if there is somewhere to go where they will be supervised).

To implement the consequences, the child should be given a choice: "It's your choice. You need to dance sensibly with X or I will move you to dance with a different partner." If conse-

Table 6.1 The Five Rs

The Five Rs	What each means	What does this look like in dance?
Rights	Being clear about what learners can expect to achieve	Everyone has the right to learn in dance. This includes performing, composing and appreciating.
Responsibilities	Establishing what the teacher expects and what learners should expect from each other	Everyone has a responsibility to make sure that others can learn to perform, compose and appreciate dance.
Rules	Having clear shared expectations about behaviour and safe practice	Listen and watch carefully, respect each other's ideas and work, respect own and each other's body, make sure everyone feels safe.
Routines	Establishing ways of working	Enter and leave the dance space properly. Know where to put belongings. Know what to wear and where to sit. Know signals to stop and listen.
Rewards	Rewarding good learning and behaviour	Have individual, group and class rewards. Use class or school systems. Establish praise, stickers, merits, certificates, postcards.

quences have to be applied, then it is important to restore and repair at the end of the lesson by sharing what happened and making it clear what will happen next time or by praising the child for improved behaviour.

> ## Task
>
> With the children, draw up golden rules for dance and create a display for the dance space.

Establishing Routines

Children are used to having classroom routines, and the same should apply to the dance space. Arrangements and expectations must be clear so that no lesson time is wasted:

- Changing: Usually children change for dance and PE in the classroom, but as they grow older, it is more appropriate for boys and girls to change separately.

- Coming and going: Children should enter and leave the dance space in a calm and orderly way so that everyone feels safe and other classes are not distracted.

- Belongings: Children need to know where to put their belongings (such as shoes and jumpers) so that they can find them quickly at the end of the lesson.

- Introduction: Start the lesson with the children sitting on the floor close to you so that they can listen and contribute to the lesson introduction.

- Transitions: Have some strategies for sending the children from sitting on the floor to the space. This might be a group at a time or you closing your eyes and counting to 10.

- Space: Remind the children to find a safe space to dance in and not to touch anyone else unless required to.

- Stopping and stillness: Dance lessons are often quite busy and noisy. Children share ideas, try out movements and give instructions. They are often excited and should always be having fun. It is therefore useful to have agreed signals for stopping and stillness. These might be the same as are used in the classroom (as long as they are transferable to a larger space) and should be appropriate for the age and stage of the children. Here are some suggested strategies:

- Raise your hand and children copy.
- Shake a tambourine or beat a tambour.
- Stop the music and signal to the children to sit down.
- Project your voice, asking children to freeze or sit and listen.

These routines will give you and the children confidence and a clear framework in which to learn.

Managing the Space

It is important to develop and vary the use of space in lessons so that children dance confidently, safely and independently. Warm-ups on the web resource provide examples of how to use the space for warming up. Step-by-step examples demonstrate how to progress the learning from sitting to standing to travelling and from standing in a static circle to using the space independently, then finding partners and working in groups. These strategies can also be applied to other parts of the lesson when children are exploring and developing movement material. Some children so enjoy the feeling of freedom and unrestricted space that they travel round the outside of the room showing lack of spatial awareness. Encouraging children to focus on making a clear floor pattern and travelling in different directions (as appropriate to the task) will develop their understanding of spatial design. Markings on the hall floor can also provide visual reminders of areas in which to dance. It is also a good idea to model how the space should be used by selecting children who are using space thoughtfully to demonstrate.

Pace and Momentum

Good pace and momentum will keep the children active and engaged. To achieve momentum, keep tasks short and build on each by adding another dimension. For instance, in Mission: Impossible, the children explore travelling on different **levels** as if they are secret agents. Having demonstrated that they are able to do this with control and coordination, they can then travel at different speeds and in different directions. They can move over, under and around imaginary obstacles; they can add a pause. The next task is to follow a partner, keeping all these aspects in mind, before developing a partner sequence that can be repeated. Opportunities to practise and refine dances are important, as is the observation of good examples or of each other. There will be times for sitting, observing and reflecting, and

Children observing each other.

child should be prepared to dance with each other regardless of ability, gender or friendship. Dance, of course, covers the activities of performing, composing and appreciating. Willingness to dance with anybody and everybody in the class is something to aspire to. It is advisable to design tasks that encourage socialising, such as warm-ups where children move around independently and on command, in which they stop and relate to the nearest child or form groups of a given number. The Meeting and Greeting dance, which starts as a warm-up (see web resource) and develops into a group dance composition, is a good example of how to achieve random groupings in a lesson. It also develops social skills.

Grouping children for dance should be fit for purpose. There may be times when you as the teacher will decide the groupings for a lesson or a series of lessons, perhaps for assessment purposes, and this is perfectly acceptable. Children who experience regular dance sessions throughout the primary years are more likely to feel comfortable dancing with each other and in mixed-sex groups, whereas if they lack confidence it is best to allow them to choose whom they dance with. One quick strategy for mixing up the class is to ask them to stand in a circle and then shout out commands to quickly change places with children across the circle if they have, for instance, a pet cat or have slept in a tent or they like macaroni and cheese, and so on. A word of warning: In a class where the boys and girls are reluctant to mix, they will end up in same-sex groupings after several tries at the "swap places" game!

the pace will be maintained if the children do the evaluating and provide the feedback, with your guidance, before further refining their dances. Appreciation activities should be short, focused and purposeful so that children are not sitting for too long. Observing and feeding back on a one-to-one, pair-to-pair or group-to-group basis are more effective uses of time than all of the class looking at one group at a time.

Structuring a lesson or a unit of work that provides opportunities for children to progress from exploring movement and creating phrases individually to composing with a partner and then combining the material in a group is particularly effective in key stage 2 because it ensures that every child contributes and has ownership of the work.

Groupings

Dance provides an opportunity for children to choose with whom they wish to learn. At the same time in order to achieve a positive learning ethos, in which there are good relationships and mutual respect, every

Key stage 2 children working well in a group.

MEETING AND GREETING DANCE

This dance provides a suitable introduction to traditional folk dance and is also an effective ice-breaker.

Age Range

Years 3 and 4 (it also works well with adults in staff training sessions)
Accompaniment: electric folk (lesson 1) and something funky or space age (lesson 2)

Instructions

Lesson 1

1. Children walk in and out of the spaces (on the beat) changing direction; they smile, make eye contact and nod to each other as they pass.

2. They continue to move around the space waving to each other as they pass, then shaking hands with each other (left or right). They are not allowed to let go of a hand until they grasp a new one.

3. Pause the action and keep hold of the last hand. This is now the partner to dance with. They face each other. Teach a sequence of 8 waves with the right hand and 8 waves with the left; 8 right-hand shakes and 8 left-hand shakes; with hands on each other's shoulders turn clockwise together for 8 counts then anti-clockwise for 8.

4. Give each other a high five and walk off alone again (this time travelling backwards). Pause and face the nearest person and repeat the wave, shake and turn pattern. Repeat several times, varying the independent travelling (walk sideways, skip or gallop).

5. Meet up in groups of four and repeat the pattern (shaking hands with the dancer opposite over or under the other pair of hands and putting arms around the dancers on either side for the turning phrase).

6. This is the working group for the rest of the lesson. Discuss different forms of greeting in other times and places. Each group chooses two and combines these to add a new section to the pattern. Share the outcomes.

This lesson provides a suitable introduction to traditional folk dance, or it can be developed as follows:

Lesson 2 (Creative Development)

1. Repeat the Meeting and Greeting dance as a warm-up (without the new additions) to form new groups of four.

2. Split into pairs and imagine you are from the planet Zog and make up an alien greeting that no one has seen before. Make sure it has a pattern and goes with the music. Add a short travel towards each other and a short travel away after the greeting.

3. Regroup in fours and teach each other the alien greeting phrases. Combine and perform the alien greeting dance as a group.

4. One dancer from each group moves to a different group to teach their alien greeting dance. Children could evaluate the effectiveness of the teaching and learning.

As far as group sizes go, by the time they are six years old, children should be able to dance cooperatively in pairs and sometimes in small groups. In key stage 2 they should develop group-working skills so that they can regularly create and perform dances in pairs and groups. Partner work is ideal because it can easily lead to working in fours, but the group size should depend on the theme. Groups of three and five can provide more dynamic relationship possibilities. Six is probably the largest group size that is manageable for any length of time in upper key stage 2.

Differentiation

This is where teachers personalise the learning by setting tasks that meet individual and group needs so that every child is challenged and is able to achieve his or her personal best. Like art, music and drama, **differentiation** in dance is often by outcome in that all the children in the class are set the same task to begin with. However, there may be times when it is necessary to adapt tasks to meet different needs. Broadly speaking, you can achieve differentiation by limiting or extending the following:

- Action content of the task (e.g., select two, three or four actions from the word bank to explore and create a sequence)
- Spatial content of the task (e.g., all stay on the spot, most also add a change of level, some also travel across the space)
- Group size (some children may find it easier to work in a smaller group or with a partner)
- Adult support
- Choreographic complexity (e.g., "Now that you have good unison, can you include canon and action and reaction?")
- Performance skills (e.g., "All of you will work on timing, and most of you will also work on focus; this group will also work on extension.")

Limiting choices can sometimes provide more challenge than offering free choice. In recent times pupil choice and independent learning have been a focus in schools. In dance this can be difficult but not impossible to manage. Whilst starting points and accompaniment are normally selected by the teacher, children with dance experience can make choices about the size of the group they work in, the stimulus for their dance (such as a choice from a variety of pictures or poems) and the form and structure of their dance.

Non-Participants

There should be no such thing as a non-participant in dance (would non-participation be allowed in literacy lessons?). If a child is unable to join in for health reasons, he or she can still be involved in composing and appreciating tasks. The child could be given recording or reporting tasks, for example, by making a note of the dance vocabulary or the actions used; sketch the body and group shapes or pathways; or use a video camera to record children's work. Or they could be "artistic directors" to specific groups and give advice or feedback on performance. Children should not be punished by not allowing them to join in (for instance, if they have not brought their kit). Dance is an entitlement for all, and every step should be taken to ensure participation.

On rare occasions, children may refuse to take part because they are unsure of what is expected or lack confidence. This requires a low-key approach. The strategies mentioned previously would be appropriate ways to engage them until they feel reassured. For younger children, sitting close to you for the introduction and joining in with sitting and standing activities often build confidence to participate.

Dance Space

In an ideal world, the dance space will have adequate room for travelling and jumping and for groups to create dances. Most school halls have an appropriate environment providing the floor is clean and without obstacles. If the space is restricted, activities must be planned that do not cover space such as warming up on the spot. The children could work half a class at a time while the others observe and give feedback. They could be encouraged to watch and remember so as to save time when it is their turn. Dancing outdoors can be fun, and there are two specific contexts where this can be effective. The first is when the dance is created to respond to the environment, such as an off-site visit to a natural environment, formal gardens, a sculpture park or in response

Some children find it easier to work with adult support.

to the shapes and designs of buildings. The second is a traditional folk dance festival or event. In either context, there needs to be clearly delineated performance space and established signals for stopping and stillness because voices do not carry so far outdoors. You should ensure that the ground is reasonably level and free of obstacles, and remember that constant vibration on the earth brings the worms to the surface because they think it's raining! More details about dance spaces are in chapter 9.

Dance often suffers from lack of visual display. Most school halls have a wipe-clean board that can be used to support the learning in the lesson by displaying the learning outcome and success criteria and the dance vocabulary. A dance display board with photos of professional dancers, word banks and children's writing and drawings will raise the profile of dance in the school. A portable mobile displaying key movement words constructed from wire coat hangers and pegs makes a useful display tool for the dance space.

Role of the Adult

As the teacher, you play many roles in a dance lesson, including leader, manager, organiser, demonstrator, director and assessor. It is not necessary to be a dancer in order to teach dance. But enthusiasm for dance, knowledge of the children and good subject knowledge are of paramount importance. The main thing to remember is that you are the facilitator and enabler so that the children become the choreographers.

Learning support or teaching assistants are like gold because they can provide invaluable support for individuals and groups of children providing they are confident of their role in the lesson. Good communication and shared expectations are important, and the assistant may have particular skills that can be used, such as leading the warm-up so that you can observe and assess the children. Helpers should be sensitive to individual needs and provide minimal assistance so that children become independent learners.

Dance artists can be so stimulating and exciting to work with. Again, communication and shared expectations are important (see chapter 9). Dance artists often come with no knowledge of the children; therefore, their expectations are often high. It never ceases to amaze teachers how well children rise to the occasion! The role of the dance artists is primarily to share their specialism with the children and their teacher. They may require support with aspects of management such as behaviour, especially if they do not know the children.

Inclusive Practice

An important fundamental of inclusion is to ensure that each young person is able to participate from a comfortable and safe position that optimises their involvement.

Gargrave and Trotman 2003, p.32.

The terms *comfortable* and *safe* include both physical and emotional security. Whether children have physical disabilities or learning difficulties, many of the teaching approaches are the same:

- Recognise that children develop at different rates and in different ways.
- Know the children. Find out what they can do, watch how they move and plan accordingly. Seek professional advice and guidance if necessary.
- Make sure everyone in the class understands and agrees with the rules for taking part and that they share responsibility for safety (emotional and physical).
- Be clear about the role of other adults in the room (teaching assistants or supporters). Are they there to join in and help, or is independence to be encouraged?
- Communicate with careful and sensitive choice of language. For instance, if there is a child with impaired mobility, the children could be asked to move around rather than walk around the space.
- Value the process of creating dance. Focus on the quality of movement and on performing with good focus. Give the children ownership of the work and respect individuality.
- Adapt tasks to provide challenge for every individual and so that each can achieve success.

Children should feel confident in their preferred way of moving. You can then encourage them to extend their movement range and repertoire by exploring and developing further possibilities. Dance provides an ideal context for the development of fundamental movement skills (body management, locomotion and object control). But you are most likely not a movement or dance therapist, so it is important to find out how best to support the work of physiotherapists and other professionals.

Physical Disabilities

To enhance the dance experience for children with physical disabilities, first consider the space. Is there room for children with mobility impairments or motor disorders to travel, turn and stop? Is the space free of obstructions for children with visual, mobility or coordination impairments? A zoned space could provide a safe area for a child to explore and develop movement skills and aid orientation. For children using mobility aids, you need to make a decision about whether to use soft mats rather than aids—it depends on the nature of the task and the needs of the individual. You should help children to achieve and work from a balanced position whether lying, seated or standing, with or without support. Strategies for inclusion include the following:

- Adapt travelling movements for sitting or standing.
- Provide frequent intervals of rest.
- Limit conditions, use alternative body parts or focus on the most mobile parts of the body.
- Provide partners who can lead or guide the movement.
- Provide props, such as pieces of fabric, streamers or hoops, to extend the range of motion.
- Break down tasks into simple steps.
- Limit the size of groups.
- Share with the class examples of work from inclusive dance companies, such as Candoco (UK), Stopgap (UK), Dancing Wheels (USA) and Axis (USA).

Children with visual impairments will need a safe space in which to move. They will respond to tactile stimuli that have texture and shape. Movements can be guided manually by the light touch of an adult or partner, and their hands can draw designs such as pathways and body shapes so that they become familiar with these. Clear use of spoken vocabulary and a recognised sound such as jingling bells to signal location will also help. Children with hearing impairments need to be able to see your face and mouth and to read your facial expressions. Clear demonstration is also important, and you can use word or picture cues to describe phrases or dance structures. They will respond best to music with a percussive beat and live percussion (they are often able to feel the music's beat through a suspended wooden floor) and will enjoy creating their own body percussion by clapping and tapping.

Learning Difficulties

This term covers a wide range of mild to severe and complex needs. Movement memory can be a barrier to learning, and children with learning difficulties may not have the refined movement memory required for abstract dance, but they will benefit from repeating sequences or movement patterns, such as those of social and traditional dance forms. Narrative dance forms also provide story lines and images that aid movement memory. Here are strategies for inclusion:

- Clear, short instructions
- Good practical demonstration
- Material broken down into manageable steps
- Plenty of time to repeat and refine
- Encouragement at working at a slower pace and starting simply
- Visual prompts such as notated movements, shapes and patterns using images, words, stick figures or designs as a memory aid
- Positive and encouraging feedback
- A supportive partner

Autistic children will find it easier to join in if you explain in advance what they will be doing. Their **personal space** should be respected, and it is a good idea to recognise and capitalise on their preferred movement patterns.

For all children with learning difficulties, remember to aim for quality rather than quantity by focusing on the quality of the movement and the creative outcome. Provide conditions and restrictions. For instance, choose two actions rather than three or four; create a phrase on the spot rather than travelling; and restrict the number of dancers in the group and keep the task short, for instance, fill 8 counts of music instead of 16.

> ### Task
> Identify the children in your class or school with physical disabilities and significant learning difficulties and discuss how their needs will be met in dance.

Talented and Gifted Children

Gifted and talented children have the potential to develop significantly beyond what is expected for their ages. Gifted children have been defined as those with exceptional ability in one or more academic subjects, and talented children are those with exceptional skills in practical areas such as art, music, sport and dance. Schools have a responsibility to identify gifted and talented children and to make appropriate provision for them. In dance, a talented child may demonstrate exceptional ability in one or more of the activities of performing, composing and appreciating. Some children may be exceptionally talented in a specific dance style such as ballroom, ballet or disco. Characteristics of talented young dancers include the following:

Schools have an obligation to recognise and celebrate talent in dance.

- Keen and enthusiastic
- Attentive and focused for lengths of time
- Propensity to ask questions and enjoy discussing dance
- Confident use of space
- Confident in working alone but also enjoy working collaboratively
- Enjoyment of physical challenge and tackling difficult tasks
- Responsive to corrections and constructive feedback
- Good movement memory
- Quick to learn, copy and reproduce

What steps can you take to ensure that talented young dancers' needs are met? There are three contexts to consider:

Dance Lesson

- Set tasks that provide challenge (see previous section on differentiation).
- Set tasks to develop skills in complementary areas that the talented child may not be so confident or skilled in. For instance, highly skilled performers may find compositional tasks challenging.
- Provide breadth and balance of dance experiences across the year (e.g., different starting points, accompaniment, styles and types of dance).
- It is not cliché to ask a talented child to teach a partner or small group in a lesson because teaching requires high-order thinking skills in order to deconstruct a skill.

- Find opportunities for a talented child to contribute to the learning, such as by creating a sequence or chorus for a class dance or by demonstrating particular skills.

School

- Ensure that colleagues and the coordinator responsible for talented and gifted pupils are aware of a talented child.
- Ensure that the child's name is placed on the talented and gifted register and find out what the school policy states.
- At the end of the year, ensure smooth transition to the next class or school by sharing information with relevant staff.
- Ensure that the school recognises and celebrates talent in dance, such as by providing opportunities for dance in assemblies and concerts and, if appropriate, making provision for talented young dancers to participate in suitable projects and extra-curricular activities.

Community

- Recognise and celebrate talented young dancers' achievements out of school. They might be achieving high standards in private dance classes or community dance groups.
- Liaise with parents and carers to find out how the school can best support them; they may not realise how talented their child is.
- Signpost parents and child to the oppor-

tunities for dance out of school, such as classes or projects in the community, junior associate schemes run by renowned ballet schools and access to live professional performances. Contact local dance agencies and arts organisations, local dance or arts venues, local authorities and Youth Dance England.

> ## Task
>
> Which children in your class or school are identified as talented young dancers? How do you provide for them?

Boys and Dance

Dance is the one subject where stereotyping and prejudice towards boys and men participating are most likely to rise to the surface. Prejudice is likely to be found more among adults (including parents and school staff members) than children, however. There are several historical and cultural reasons that contribute to stereotyping and homophobic attitudes to boys and men who dance. Whilst in some cultures it is acceptable for men to dance, dance as an art form in which the expression of feelings is central is not considered to be masculine. Many adults lack awareness of contemporary dance (with its contemporary themes, naturally based and high-energy movement and unisex approach) and often associate dancing with classical ballet (even though they might not watch it) in which men and women are perceived to play distinct roles. Another factor to stereotyping is the way in which dance has been delivered in secondary schools. Dance has been mainly taught by female teachers to girls as part of a PE programme whilst boys played sport. This has been perpetuated through many generations of pupils who are now parents and teachers.

Boys and girls *are* different. They have different developmental rates, different learning preferences and preferred ways of moving; a few minutes observing children in the playground will illustrate the latter. Rachel Hutchinson, former head of dance at South Dartmoor Community College in Devon, played a significant role in developing boys' dance in her school, the South West region and in sports colleges (schools with specialist sport status) in the 1990s. Although the project was based in a large secondary school, the evidence and powerful outcomes resonate in any age group. The aim was to promote a positive image of boys dancing and engage more boys in

Boys performing with good energy and focus.

dance throughout the school. Following a residency with Rambert Dance Company, a boys' performance group (including targeted students with behavioural, social, personal and attendance issues) was formed that toured other sports colleges with performances and workshops. The boys chose to explore physical strength, strong lines, fast and challenging movement and use of props. The project had a significant impact on the boys' personal, social and academic development. It enriched lives and ultimately raised attainment. Improvements were noted in physical and social skills, self-confidence, motivation, attendance, thinking, learning, concentration, communication, team-working skills and perceptions of dance. Rachel observed the way in which boys and girls learned in dance in her school and found typical preferences as shown in table 6.2 (Jarvis 2005, p. 18).

Boys also enjoy physical contact, using the floor and working in narrative or dance drama forms but can find intricate step patterns challenging. It is vital to address negative attitudes in the class and throughout the school to boys' dancing and to provide a safe ethos for physical expression. It is equally important not to overcompensate for boys by continually finding

Table 6.2   Typical Learning Preferences of Boys and Girls

Boys like	Girls like
Structure	Working with stimuli
Closed and specific tasks	Open-ended tasks
Pace, energy and physical challenge	Opportunities to be creative and imaginative
Competition	Appreciation tasks
Short and directed units of work	Flexibility in a clear framework

themes and content that will appeal to them, such as robots, space travel, machines and sports, because these could reinforce stereotypes. Both boys and girls need to be challenged by dance material in a range of styles and types of dance.

Here are strategies for improving attitudes and engaging boys in dance:

- Select material that is relevant to both sexes and that encourages a full range of actions and dynamics.

- Capitalise on popular dance culture such as in TV programmes featuring dance competitions in a range of styles; these provide useful resources for material.

- Promote male role models (dance teachers, performers and choreographers) by displaying photos, using dance DVDs and accessing visiting dancers and dance companies. These could be students from a local secondary school or college.

- Set tasks that provide choices and achieve a balance between open-ended and directed tasks. For example, in A Winning Dance (see web resource) the children have a freestyle section where they can use their strengths.

- Raise the profile of dance in school by making it more public, such as showing class dances in assemblies (process and product) and ensuring that boys are represented in dance performances and concerts.

- Raise the profile of dance with governors and parents by communicating what dance is and its educational value.

Task

What can you or your school do to promote positive images of boys and men in dance?

Summary

The many practical ideas and strategies in this chapter will enable you to create a positive ethos for learning in dance and meet the needs of all the children in your care so that each child receives his or her entitlement to dance and makes progress and achieves success.

Assessing Dance

This chapter provides a practical approach to assessing dance. It explores the relationship between assessment, teaching and learning and examines what formative assessment and summative assessment look like in dance. The chapter provides expectations for performance, composition and appreciation at four stages: reception, year 2, year 4 and year 6. These expectations can be used in supporting planning and also for formative and summative assessment purposes.

Assessment is integral to effective teaching and learning, and it should be neither arduous nor mysterious. Teachers continually assess children in order to decide next steps, set the next task, plan the next lesson, decide the content for the next unit of work and evaluate the effectiveness of their teaching. Assessment in dance focuses on what the children understand and can do as they perform, compose and appreciate dance. Because dance is largely practical, it is easy to see how well children achieve in performance and composition and whether they are suitably challenged. Although most assessment will be carried out through direct observation, other effective strategies include questioning; listening to children discussing and planning dance, listening to them evaluating performance and composition and providing feedback to others.

The two types of assessment—**formative** and **summative**—are mutually dependent. Assessment is neither inherently formative nor summative; the timing and how the information is used decide which form it takes. Formative assessment, or assessment for learning, relates to ongoing assessment by both children and adults during the lesson, whereas summative assessment relates to the end-of-unit, end-of-year or key stage judgements about attainment.

Teacher questioning a child about dance.

Assessment for Learning (Formative Assessment)

Assessment for learning is "the process of seeking and interpreting evidence for use by learners and their teachers to decide where the learners are in their learning, where they need to go and how best to get there."

Assessment Reform Group 2002.

Assessment for learning is underpinned by the knowledge that ability is not fixed and that every child can make progress. As well as being essential to teaching and learning, assessment for learning

- involves sharing learning goals with the children;
- helps children understand what they are aiming for, what counts as good work and what the success criteria are;
- involves children in self-assessment and peer assessment so they take more responsibility for their own learning;

- provides feedback about the qualities of the work and what needs to be done to improve (to which children should respond actively); and

- involves teachers and children reviewing and reflecting on achievement.

Sharing Learning Goals With Children

Some schools focus on both learning objectives (what the children will be learning) and learning outcomes (what they know, understand or are able to do by the end of the lesson).

Sharing the learning outcomes.

A more economic and equally effective approach is to focus on learning outcomes alone. One to three learning outcomes per lesson are adequate; you should share these at the start and during the lesson and for reflection and self-evaluation at the end. Phrase the outcomes in clear, simple and child-friendly language and use them as a basis for questioning and feedback. Learning outcomes should relate to knowledge, understanding and skills so that by the end of a lesson children would

- know that . . .

- understand how . . .

- be able to . . .

- explore and refine strategies for . . .

Performance, composition and appreciation provide the basis for learning outcomes. Three examples are as follows:

- By the end of this lesson we will have improved our street dance performance for sharing in assembly (performance).

- By the end of today's lesson we will have created a short group dance based on one verse of a poem about winter (composition).

- By the end of the lesson we will know some facts about South African gumboot dancing and be able to create a short gumboot sequence with a partner using two different rhythms (appreciation and composition).

It is also important that children understand why they are learning—in other words, what is the relevance of the learning outcomes to their everyday lives? Learning goals include individual and group targets that might relate to more generic performance, composition and appreciation (or social and behavioural) outcomes.

Helping Children Know and Recognise the Standards

This requires agreeing and sharing clear success criteria related to the learning outcome. For instance, for the first outcome listed previously, the success criteria might be good timing, good focus and strong, rhythmic movement. It is most effective when children arrive at the success criteria themselves in response to a teacher's question: "What will a good street dance performance look like?" Seeing good examples of work is also crucial—this can be achieved by an adult or other children modelling what is expected and by looking at the work of other children or professionals on film. Another useful strategy to consider is that when sharing work with a wider audience (such as to another class or in assembly) teachers and children share the process as well as the product so that everyone understands and appreciates the steps to success in dance.

Peer Assessment and Self-Assessment

Physical education and dance teachers are good at this because it has been an inherent part of effective teaching for many years. **Peer assessment** and self-assessment improve learning by engaging the children with the quality of their own and each other's work and in reflecting on how it can be improved and enhanced. Children learn well from each other, especially in a supportive environment where they can talk, discuss, suggest and appraise. **Self-assessment** encourages children to take responsibility for their own progress and promotes independent learning. However, assessment needs to be developed and practised. It requires you to model by using clear success criteria, effective questioning and suggestions for improvement (next steps). For example, using the third learning outcome listed previously (gumboot dance), pairs could observe each other to evaluate the practical task; look for rhythms, order and repetition; give feedback and offer suggestions for improvement.

Children learn well from each other in a supportive environment.

They could also reflect on what they have learned about gumboot dancing (from practical experience and also from watching a video clip) and tell a partner three things they know. Success criteria could be printed on separate cards for each child, pair or group to arrange in an order from "best" to "needs improvement." These evaluations could be recorded as photos.

Children need time during the lesson to reflect and also opportunities to talk about what they have achieved, what they found challenging and what they want to improve. Video is a great aid to self-assessment (it takes a while for children to get used to looking at themselves dancing objectively, however). Self-evaluation sheets for written reflection bring another dimension to the learning. As well as being evidence of learning, written evaluation takes dance into the classroom and reinforces reading and writing skills. Alternatively, children could record their reflections using diagrams such as stick figures. The three examples of self-evaluation that follow are different approaches to self-evaluation at different stages in the primary phase.

Providing Feedback

Your feedback to children in dance lessons will be mainly verbal, regular and interactive. Feedback might be directed to individuals or groups, or it could be indirect in that children hear what you are telling others and reflect on and respond to what you said. Your comments should recognise effort and achievement and also be positive and constructive. Feedback should also be developmental in that it provides details for the next steps for improvement or the way forward. An example is "Well done. Your group dance based on the

winter poem is beginning to look very effective. You linked the actions together smoothly, and you had a strong starting position. The next step is to think about how you use the space. With more variety in levels and directions, you will have a really good group dance." This models how to give constructive feedback.

Reviewing and Reflecting on Assessment

This is about sharing assessment information and next steps with the children. It could comprise looking at the outcomes of summative assessment (i.e., how well they achieved in the last unit of work). You could share this information with them and also use it to adapt the teaching for the next unit of work, plan the unit of work and decide the next steps for the children.

Summative Assessment

Summative assessment is carried out periodically to judge how well children are doing. This information might be reported in terms of levels and set alongside national standards or expectations so that attainment can be evaluated against that of other children of the same age and can be used to track progress over time. In dance it might comprise end-of-unit, end-of-year and end-of-key-stage assessments against levels or descriptors. You could report this information to colleagues, parents and carers and also to teachers of the next stage or the next school. There are early learning goals for physical and creative skills for assessment at the end of the early years and foundation stage and, at the time of this writing,

YEAR 2 SELF-EVALUATION

Name: _____ Date: _____

Highlight what you are good at.

I am good at

Moving slowly	Stopping	Dancing on my own
Moving quickly	Jumping	Remembering movements
Balancing	Following a partner	Talking about dance

YEAR 4 SELF-EVALUATION

The Calabash Children

Name: _____ Date: _____

Select phrases to write in the table.

Creating sequences from everyday actions	Keeping time with other dancers
Sharing ideas	Remembering sequences
Dancing with a partner	Remembering the whole dance
Dancing in a group	Performing to others
Keeping time with the music	Making improvements

Things I find easy	Things I can improve

What I enjoyed most about The Calabash Children:

YEAR 6 SELF-EVALUATION

Rock 'n' Roll

Name: _____ Date: _____

Use traffic light colours (green, amber, red) to indicate your strengths and targets.

- Sense of style (energy and rhythm)
- Control and coordination
- Step patterns
- Timing
- Partner work
- Creative freestyle ideas
- Good transitions

Three facts I know about rock 'n' roll:

1.

2.

3.

the statutory expectations are for schools in England to report on attainment in the foundation subjects at the end of each key stage. In the past there have been generic attainment targets and age-related levels for PE (but not specifically for dance) that focus on acquiring skills, adapting skills, evaluating performance and knowledge and understanding fitness and health.

Over recent years dance specialists have worked together to develop appropriate year-by-year expectations for dance. Youth Dance England (2011) developed a framework for teaching, learning and assessment for ages 3 to 19. The expectations provided at the end of this chapter have been adapted from this framework. This is available from the NDTA at www.ndta.org.uk≠publications≠the=dance=frame=work=complete=package. You are not expected to keep detailed records of individual pupils' achievement in every subject. Providing that units of work (medium-term plans) have clear learning outcomes, it would be sufficient to assume that most in the class achieve these and to make a note of those children who exceed or struggle with them. It is important to record and report on achievement in dance because often certain children who struggle with other subjects and sports have strengths in dance that should be celebrated. It is also a good strategy for promoting the subject and giving it status. Reports to parents and carers should evaluate children's progress and achievement in performance, composition and appreciation rather than merely describing the dances they have participated in.

How Do Children Develop in Dance?

Some knowledge and understanding of how children develop in dance is necessary in order to plan appropriate and suitably challenging dance activities. In her book *Dancing to Learn* (1989), Mary Lowden analysed progression in movement from year to year in the primary phase. The following descriptions are summaries of her observations.

Understanding of Dance

With five-year-olds there is little difference between normal activity and dancing in that movements are natural and unrefined. By the time they are seven, children have a more objective view of dance and have movement ideas (i.e., they can imagine dancing) without having to actually move. Eleven-year-olds can grasp more abstract dance ideas, select movements to communicate meaning and use symbolism. They can explore different types of dance and are proficient in various dance styles.

Movement Skills

Movement on the floor is part of the natural vocabulary of five-year-olds. They explore actions, dynamics and space as a natural response to their environment and can understand and achieve change and contrast in movements. Seven-year-olds control and manage their

Movement on the floor is natural for five-year-olds.

Seven-year-olds control and manage their bodies well.

bodies quite well. They recognise, compare and perform differences in movement and have developed a sense of performance. They can remember, repeat and refine movement phrases. Nine-year-olds have acquired and developed a wider range of skills and can perform subtle changes in actions, dynamics and space. Eleven-year-olds move fluently with good control, coordination and extension. They remember and accurately repeat complex sequences and are willing to take physical chances.

Composition

Five-year-olds are able to make simple movement choices. By the time they are seven, they are able to select, sequence and adapt movement material. Nine-year-olds can try out and adapt movement ideas and order movement phrases and sequences into simple compositional forms. Eleven-year-olds can compose short complete dances that have clear form and compositional devices.

Working With Others

Five-year-olds share space and work alongside each other, but they dance individually. They pick up cues in body language of others and are quick to respond to it. Seven-year-olds can lead and follow in pairs and small groups, and they understand the concept of helping each other. Nine-year-olds contribute to group dances and are able to direct and be directed. By the time

they are 11, they can work in various-sized groups, taking on different roles. They are able to support each other sensitively.

Expectations for Dance

The expectations that follow are based on what can be expected for the majority of children at each stage. To hold high expectations in dance, it is recommended that teachers of years 1, 3 and 5 aim for the following year's expectations. They provide guidance for planning units and schemes of work and for assessing children's dance performance, composition and appreciation. A unit of work would focus on perhaps three or four of the expectations (specific expectations are identified for each unit on the web resource), and experiencing a range of dances across one or two years should enable most children to meet the performance, composition and appreciation expectations for their age. These expectations would be useful when considering which children are struggling and those who are gifted and talented. They could be used to plot progress and decide next steps, but it is not suggested that every child be assessed against each statement. A sample of children (of different abilities in dance) could be assessed to provide an overview of the attainment of the whole class. Tables 7.1 to 7.3 will also help you explain dance expectations to parents and governors and could be included in the school's dance policy.

Eleven-year-olds are proficient in styles.

Table 7.1   Expectations for Performance

Aspect	Foundation	Year 2	Year 4	Year 6
Physical skills	Travel, turn, jump, gesture and balance with a degree of control and coordination.	Perform a range of actions with control and coordination.	Perform a range of actions with control, coordination and body tension.	Perform a range of actions with control, coordination, body tension and fluency.
Expressive skills	Show character and expression; match movements to music.	Show expression through face, posture, action and dynamics; show good awareness of others.	Perform expressively using dynamic qualities to illustrate the dance idea; show sensitivity to others.	Perform expressively using dynamic qualities to illustrate the dance idea; show sensitivity to others.
Movement memory	Remember and repeat short movement patterns.	Perform short dances within a given structure.	Remember movement phrases and short dances.	Remember phrases and dances.
Presenting dance	Move with confidence and perform to others.	Perform short dances to others.	Perform short dances with a sense of audience.	Perform with focus and projection to an audience.
Safe practice	Show an awareness of self and others; recognise changes in their bodies when active.	Know that they should prepare for dance and move safely.	Understand the importance of warming up, cooling down and moving safely.	Understand the importance of warming up, cooling down and moving safely; lead warm-up and cool-down activities in small groups.

Table 7.2 Expectations for Composition

	Foundation	Year 2	Year 4	Year 6
Respond	Respond spontaneously through movement to a variety of stimuli.	Respond to different stimuli.	Respond imaginatively to different stimuli.	Confidently and imaginatively respond to and research a range of dance ideas.
Explore	Explore and move with appropriate actions in response to stimuli and dance ideas.	Confidently explore actions that express dance ideas.	Confidently and imaginatively explore and experiment with different actions in response to dance ideas.	Confidently and imaginatively explore and experiment with different actions in response to dance ideas.
Create and select	Select movements such as starting and finishing positions.	Choose appropriate actions, space, dynamics and relationships.	Create and select appropriate actions, space, dynamics and relationships.	Create and select appropriate actions, space, dynamics and relationships.
Develop	Explore how movements can be changed.	Develop actions by using dynamics and space and with a partner.	Develop phrases by using actions, dynamics and space and with a partner or small group.	Develop movement material using actions, dynamics, space and relationships to create more complex phrases and short dances.
Link	Link movements together.	Link actions to create dance phrases and short dances within a given structure.	Link actions together to create short dances.	Link actions to create dance phrases and dances.
Structure	Make decisions about beginnings and endings.	Recognise movement patterns and the overall structure of a dance.	Show clear beginnings, middles and endings and use simple compositional devices such as repetition and contrast.	Use compositional devices such as unison, canon, repetition, contrast and climax.
Contribute	Suggest actions.	Discuss and share dance ideas with a partner.	Contribute and share dance ideas in pairs and small groups.	Confidently discuss and share dance ideas in pairs, in groups and with the class.
Use accompaniment	Respond spontaneously to a range of accompaniment.	Interpret accompaniment through actions and dynamics.	Respond appropriately to a range of accompaniment.	Respond to a range of accompaniment showing awareness of subtle changes in tempo, rhythm and instrumentation.

Table 7.3 Expectations for Appreciation

	Foundation	Year 2	Year 4	Year 6
Describe, interpret and evaluate dance	Use simple words to talk about what they see, do and feel in dance.	Describe and interpret what they see, do and feel in dance using a developing vocabulary.	Describe and interpret what they see, do and feel in dance using appropriate dance language.	Describe, interpret and evaluate what they see, do and feel in dance using appropriate dance language.
Describe, interpret and evaluate aspects of production	Talk about dances that they watch.	Describe and interpret aspects of production such as costume and accompaniment.	Describe and interpret aspects of production such as costume, accompaniment and physical setting.	Describe, interpret and evaluate aspects of production such as costume, accompaniment, physical setting and lighting.
Give and respond to feedback	State preferences when looking at others dance and respond to feedback.	Respond to feedback and give feedback to others using success criteria.	Respond to feedback and give effective and constructive feedback that reflects the success criteria.	Respond to feedback and know how to improve performance and composition; give constructive feedback to others.
Wider knowledge of dance	Enjoy watching people dance.	Enjoy watching people dance in a range of contexts.	Have a basic understanding of styles of dance.	Understand that dance has many forms and styles and that people dance for different reasons.

Summary

Assessment is an integral part of effective teaching and learning. Formative assessment involves the children every step of the way. Assessment for learning strategies encourages children to take more responsibility for their learning and dance, and teachers are familiar with peer assessment and self-assessment as learning tools. The agreed expectations for dance provide clear guidance for planning lessons, units and schemes of work and ensure that children's dance experience is sufficiently broad. You can use these expectations for making summative assessments of attainment and setting targets for progression.

Dance and the Curriculum

This chapter looks at dance's relationship with each curriculum subject and the ways in which they can enhance and support the other. Ideas and suggestions in this chapter, including references to units of work on the web resource, will inspire and stimulate you to develop imaginative and meaningful curriculum links and ideas.

Chapter 1 looked at dance in the curriculum, dance's relationship with the arts and PE and how children learn in and through dance. So far this book has focused on learning *in* dance (the knowledge, understanding and skills of performance, composition and appreciation). Learning *through* dance involves using it as a medium through which children learn in other curriculum areas, topics and themes. By planning dance activities as part of the whole curriculum, you can explore links and enhance learning whilst ensuring progression in performance, composition and appreciation.

As well as providing links to a wide range of subjects and curriculum areas, dance can enhance and enrich children's spiritual, moral, social and cultural development. Dance promotes spiritual development by helping children develop their sense of self and their own unique potential. They develop awareness of their strengths and weaknesses as dancers and positive attitudes to achieve and improve. In dance, children have a unique opportunity to express and communicate their feelings and their ideas about themselves and the world through a non-verbal medium. Many of the stories and poems used to inspire dance explore moral issues. In dances based on such stories children explore the idea of right and wrong, forgiveness and concern for others. Dance is essentially a social activity where children learn to cooperate, collaborate and be responsible team members as they compose and rehearse their dances. Dance is also essentially a cultural activity in which children develop an understanding of their own and others' cultural traditions. Dance also provides opportunities to engage in cultural experiences when watching professional

Dance helps children develop their sense of self.

dance on DVD or in live performances or participating in workshops and performances.

Creative Curriculum

The 2003 government publication *Excellence and Enjoyment* (DfES 2003) encourages schools to be creative and innovative in their teaching in order to provide a rich and varied learning experience beyond the national curriculum entitlement. Many schools used this opportunity to take a fresh look at their curricula, and the term *creative curriculum* is now commonplace. Schools are encouraged to build on and celebrate what makes them unique, such as their locality, the wider community and staff specialisms. Teachers can confidently respond to the children's interests and take advantage of topical affairs and issues. Curriculum planning begins with the skills (subject based or generic) to be developed, and the curriculum content is then selected to support these.

The creative curriculum encourages teachers to make meaningful links between subjects in order to strengthen and streamline learning whilst respecting the hierarchy of learning in each subject. Many schools use a thematic approach to teaching and learning that supports children's natural curiosity and stimulates their creativity. Knowledge and skills are developed and expressed through a range of media, and the creative arts play an effective role. The dance ideas in this chapter relate to curriculum themes and topics that schools already are familiar with. Figure 8.1 illustrates dance's links to other subjects.

Numeracy
- Pattern, sequence, number
- Positional language
- Shape and space: pathways, body and group shapes, formations
- Orientation and direction

Science
- Life processes and living things: body; movement; fitness and health; warming up and cooling down; animals and environments
- Physical processes: electricity, forces and motion, light, solar system
- Materials and properties: squash, bend, stretch, freeze, melt

Art and design
- Visual design: pathways, shapes, formations
- Colour: dynamics
- Compositional elements
- Drawing, painting, sculpture, print, collage, textiles, photos as stimuli
- Character, mood, events, colour, shape, symbolism

Religious education
- Worship, celebration, festivals (e.g., Holi, Diwali, Christmas)
- Expression of values and beliefs: music, art, dance, stories, artefacts, symbolism
- Cultural diversity
- Bible and creation stories
- Pilgrimages and journeys

Literacy
- Words, phrases, instructions, headlines, poems and stories as stimuli
- Speaking and listening: composing and appreciating dance
- Reading: responding to text
- Writing: reviews, evaluations, lists, instructions and imaginative writing inspired by dance
- Develop and extend vocabulary

Drama
- Time, space and movement
- Dance-drama, narrative form
- Body management, spatial awareness, expression and character
- Aspects of production: props, costume, set and lighting

Music
- Auditory aspect of dance
- The shared dimension of time
- Compositional and musical elements
- Stimulus or accompaniment
- Types and styles
- Musicality
- Dance and music relationships, creating both together

PSHE and citizenship
- Themes: friendship, bullying, diversity, inclusion, social and moral dilemmas, issues
- Learning and social skills, empathy
- Physical and emotional well-being

Design and technology
- Design and make products that link to dance ideas (e.g., puppets, robots, machines)
- Design and make costumes, accessories, props and models of stage sets

PE
- Fundamental movement skills
- Warming up and cooling down; dance as a healthy activity
- Games, swimming and athletics as stimuli

Geography
- How people live
- Maps, transport, journeys
- Places: other lands, other cultures, settlements, locations
- Patterns and processes: climate, weather, water, erosion
- Environmental issues: pollution, recycling, drought

History
- Dances of different times
- Social and cultural diversity
- The lives of other people: work, rest and play
- Significant events
- Source material: poems, paintings, stories, myths, legends, artefacts

ICT
- Research ideas and collect information
- Record dances: notation, diagrams, words, photos, film
- Create, compose and edit accompaniment
- ICT as a stimulus: cyber speak, computer games, mobile phones

Figure 8.1 Dance's links to other subjects.

Dance and Literacy

Many forms of written word can inspire dance; in turn, dance provides an effective context and experience on which to draw for literacy. Essentially both subjects are about communication—one verbal and the other non-verbal—and each requires a developing and expanding vocabulary. At a simplistic level, in dance actions are similar to verbs; dynamics are similar to adverbs and adjectives. Awareness of this concept helps in creating word banks, exploring the meanings of words and exploring movement material with the children.

Poems and stories provide a range of stimuli and starting points for dance. Not every story or poem will be suitable for use in dance, but those that contain actions, characters, adventures, journeys and contrasting environments often are. For example, the story *Where the Wild Things Are* by Maurice Sendak takes the children on a journey from the confines of Max's bedroom, through a forest, across an ocean to the island where the wild things live; each episode provides a different dance idea. Poetry shares many elements with dance; these include structure, phrasing, rhythm, pattern and often repetition. The classic poem *Jabberwocky* by Lewis Carroll provides all of these as well as an epic adventure.

Self-assessment sheets encourage reading and writing.

Words and phrases (written or spoken) also provide starting points for dance, from random action words as used in the Chance Dance unit to phrases and images in the poem The Loner by Julie Holder. Consider also newspaper headlines, instructions and well-known sayings as starting points for dance. Seemingly simple instructions for tying a shoelace demonstrated and spoken aloud by one partner and written down by another can stimulate an imaginative abstract duo based on cross, wrap, pull, loop, tuck, fold and wind.

Exploring a stimulus, composing partner or group dances and evaluating them require a considerable amount of speaking and listening through group discussion and interaction. Composing a group dance requires children to contribute ideas, listen, consider, explain, negotiate and make decisions. Evaluating the work of others requires careful consideration and choice of language.

Dance supports reading when text is used as a starting point or when children research ideas in books or on the Internet. It reinforces patterns of sound and sequences of events, providing unique opportunities to respond imaginatively to text. Creative and imaginative writing can be stimulated by dance as children enter imaginary worlds. They could retell stories that they have danced or imagine the next episode or a different ending. Dance also provides opportunities to write lists (How many stepping words can we think of?), instructions (How to perform the Snowball dance), reports and reviews. Written self-evaluations such as the examples in the previous chapter also link dance to writing.

Units of Work With Links to Literacy

- Handa's Hen, Tiddalik, Pan Gu, The Calabash Children (stories and myths from various cultures)
- What a Week! (diary)
- Chance Dance (words)
- The Loner (poem)

Dance and Numeracy

Dance shares less obvious links with numeracy, but there are nonetheless significant ways in which each supports and reinforces the other. Dance can reinforce the concepts of pattern and sequence as well as reinforce number, such as by counting patterns or groups of beats. Mathematical language and concepts can be used and reinforced in dance by using positional language (over, under, behind, in front, by the side) or when creating symmetry and asymmetry. Shape and space are the main aspects that dance shares

Traditional dances reinforce learning about shape and space.

with numeracy. This can be explored though the lines, curves and right angles of pathways and the three-dimensional forms of one or more bodies. Group formations in traditional folk dances reinforce the concept of lines, circles and squares. Consider the endless possibilities and complexities of design in a square dance or quadrille. Orientation in space provides another link with dance: children can direct each other in a robot dance to travel in different directions and make quarter, half and full turns clockwise or anticlockwise.

The Snowball unit of work reinforces sequence, pattern, number and spatial design in quite a complex but satisfying way where each figure or sequence includes an additional couple until all dance in unison, followed by a change of leadership so that the repeated pattern involves the couples in a different order.

Other Units of Work With Links to Numeracy

- Handa's Hen (positional language, number, sequence)
- All Join In and Dot, Squiggle, Dash! (spatial design)

Dance and Science

There are two significant ways in which dance and science relate. The first is shared knowledge and understanding about the body, fitness and health; the second is where science topics and themes can be explored and brought to life through dance. Dance supports learning about life processes and living things because it focuses on the body, movement, respiration, circulation and health in

every dance lesson as children warm up, remain active and cool down. For young children, the naming of body parts in a warm-up or exploring how a puppet moves will reinforce scientific knowledge. Reference to what happens when warming up, safe practice in dance and why dance is a healthy activity will also reinforce scientific understanding. Marvellous Body Machine interprets the wonders of the respiratory and circulatory system by exploring breathing, the heart pumping and the journey of blood cells through movement, partner work and pathways.

Many of the physical process topics provide suitable starting points for dance: electricity, forces and motion, light and the solar system. A dance based on the electric circuit, for instance, could include circuit pathways, going and stopping, passing a current around the group, switches, resistors and powering a device. Forces and motion provide stimulating movement exploration of pushing and pulling and magnetism, and a dance idea based on machines could incorporate both electricity and forces and motion. The effects of light could be interpreted in a dance about shadows—from simple mirroring, leading and following to a more complex dance about reflection and distortion. The solar and planetary systems provide an unusual context for dance as children explore circling actions and pathways, orbiting around each other, magnifying actions as if through a telescope, near and far and weightlessness. The study of animals and their environments provides many opportunities for dance. A key stage 1 minibeast dance reinforces knowledge of a variety of insects and the ways in which they move.

Language provides a third link between dance and science. When studying materials and their properties, children are encouraged to describe ways in which materials change when heated or cooled. What better way to explore squashing, bending, stretching, twisting, freezing, melting and dissolving than through movement?

Units of Work With Links to Science

- Handa's Hen and Tiddalik (animals and their environment)
- Marvellous Body Machine (respiration and circulation)
- The Calabash Children (plant growth)
- Toys (body parts and body awareness)

Dance and Physical Education

Whether dance is perceived as a performing art or as part of the physical education (PE) programme, it provides a balanced activity that contrasts with and complements gymnastics, games, athletics, swimming and outdoor and adventurous activities (OAA). This relationship is explored in some detail in chapter 1. Dance provides the artistic, imaginative and aesthetic dimension to the PE programme. It shares fundamental movement skills with all PE activities and a common language of movement with gymnastics. Dance enables children to develop physical confidence and competence and encourages them to be active for sustained periods. It provides a range of challenging and imaginative contexts for the development of agility, balance and coordination and rich opportunities for cooperation with others. Dance requires a good space and therefore requires time tabling alongside other PE activities to ensure there is time for skills to develop and progress. In both key stages equal time should be allocated to dance, gymnastics and games, and these should be experienced each year. Swimming, athletics and OAA should be delivered as additional blocks of experience by the end of key stage 2.

The processes of performing, composing and appreciating dance relate to the key PE aspects of learning: acquiring skills, applying skills and evaluating and improving performance. Knowing why and how to warm up and cool down for dance and also that dance is a healthy choice of activity will support children's knowledge and understanding of fitness and health. On the whole, the language of PE is objective and scientific, whereas the language of dance tends to have more in common with other art forms. Remember that dance is not an alternative game. It may share similar processes to other PE activities, but it has its own body of knowledge and understanding, particularly in the area of appreciation.

Games, swimming and athletics provide starting points for creative exploration in dance. The Olympics, for instance can be interpreted in dance by developing the actions, space, dynamics and relationship of preparing for the event; running, jumping and throwing; and winning and losing. Winter Olympic activities of skiing, sledging, skating and snowboarding can also inspire dance. Diving and swimming (especially synchronised swimming) provide interesting movement material such as exploring resistance, shape and buoyancy with a partner or in a group. Games such as football can inspire a fun and energetic class dance that involves limbering up, dribbling, shooting, saving, celebrating goals and crowd responses. Tennis, cricket, basketball and surfing could be similarly interpreted in dance. PE equipment such as hoops, ropes and gymnastics ribbons can also be used to enhance and inspire dance.

Units of Work
With Links to Physical Education

- Marvellous Body Machine
- What a Week!

Dance and the Arts

Dance shares a very special relationship with art, drama and music. They have much in common, including processes, elements and terminology, but each art form is unique in that each requires the heightened use of different senses.

Art and Design

Dancers and artists have inspired each other for thousands of years. In some cultures there is little distinction between the two art forms. An example of a close relationship is the painted dancing bodies of Australian Aborigines and the highly elaborate makeup and costume of a South Asian Kathakali dancer. In Europe and America the 20th century saw close collaboration in the theatre between artists and dancers: Degas captured the movement of dancers on stage at the Paris Opera, and Picasso designed costumes and backdrops for the Ballet Russes. Children enjoy designing and creating masks, props and costumes for their own dances, and empty shoeboxes make perfect miniature stages for set design.

Dance and visual arts share the processes of developing skills and techniques (performing), developing ideas, designing and making (composing) and evaluating and analysing (appreciating). They also share the visual elements of line, shape, form and space. The design elements include pathways (air or floor), body and group shapes and arrangements or formations in space. In dance, space has a sculptural quality, and attention to positive and negative spaces (between body parts and between dancers) is similar in paintings. Colour and texture in art could be seen to relate to the dynamic qualities that colour the movement in dance. Elements of composition such as repetition, balance, contrast, climax and motif are evident in both art forms. In addition to colour and spatial design, you can consider other features such as characters, events, mood and symbolism when using art as a stimulus.

A range of two- and three-dimensional media including drawing, painting, sculpture, textiles, print and collage provide inspiring stimuli for dance, and dance can be a powerful stimulus for art work. A number of units of work in the scheme of work are inspired by paintings in various styles and from various times. In Dot, Squiggle, Dash! the children create a three-dimensional dance from abstract two-dimensional paintings by exploring mark making using different parts of the body as well as line, shape and pattern.

Developing character through facial expression, posture and movement.

Other Units of Work Inspired by Paintings

- *Umbrellas*: Renoir
- *Our Town:* Lowry

Drama

Dance and drama share the dimensions of time and space, and both employ movement, although each for a different purpose. Drama is mostly concerned with the human condition (people, their experiences and conflict and consequences), although for younger children issues and conflict might be explored through animals and other aspects of the natural world. Dance is not always about people—it might be non-narrative, abstract or based purely on movement, and it is as much about the formal qualities of movement, time and space as it is about expression, mood and meaning. Also, in dance, movement can be patterned and structured to achieve a different end. Drama generally uses speech as a medium, whereas dance communicates non-verbally, although there are times when they overlap. **Dance drama** combines elements of each in narrative form, bringing together dance design in time and space and drama's sequence of events and human situation. An example would be a dance based on *The Pied Piper of Hamelin.*

Dance can communicate specific sections or episodes of a narrative to complement or enhance the theme or text, where words alone might be inadequate. Each dance section has its own action and relationship content and dynamic and spatial design and could therefore stand alone. For example, a play about the great fire of London might include a fire dance to show how the flames spread. In a drama based on events of World War II, time and place could be established through a jitterbug dance.

Many teachers use drama as a tool for learning in other subjects. But like dance, drama has its own body of knowledge, understanding and skills. The processes of making, performing and responding in drama are similar to the dance processes of performing, composing and appreciating. Dance supports learning in drama by enabling children to manage their bodies and use space confidently; exploring the expression of mood and feeling through actions, space, dynamics and relationships; using movement to enhance the narrative (such as providing atmosphere, tension and climax); and developing character through facial expression, posture and movement. Dance and drama also share aspects of production that enhance both art forms such as lighting, set design, costume, makeup and props.

Units of Work With Links to Drama

- Tiddalik (narrative, issue based, character)
- The Calabash Children (narrative, everyday actions)
- The Loner (mood, issue based)
- Our Town (character, everyday life)
- Pan Gu (narrative, dramatic movement)
- Mission: Impossible (dramatic action, suspense)

Music

Music as accompaniment for dance is explored in detail in chapter 9. It is difficult to imagine dance without music because they share such a close relationship with music contributing to the auditory aspect of dance. Both of them share the dimension of time. Music and dance develop creativity and self-discipline, and the cultural dimension of each helps children understand themselves and others. The processes of performing, composing and appreciating music are shared with dance, and both subjects require the skills of rehearsing and performing with others. Dance provides children with rich opportunities to respond to a range of music and to develop their knowledge of musical composition.

The various types of music (orchestral, percussion, electronic and found sound) and the styles (traditional, classical, folk, pop, contemporary and jazz) provide the range and variety required for a range of dance experiences. The musical elements of structure and form are shared with dance, and the elements of pitch, duration, dynamics, tempo, rhythm, timbre and texture are what dancers respond to through movement. Music can affect the emotions by creating mood and atmosphere; it can also inspire thoughts, memories and feelings.

As a stimulus for dance, music requires children to listen carefully and respond. Spontaneous response to music through movement is an ability that very young children have and that they seem to lose as they grow older. This skill is worth maintaining and practising from time to time, such as by saying, "Show me how you move to this music." Musicality is the ability to pick out and use the unique qualities of music sensitively in both performance and composition. It can be enhanced by providing children with a rich range of appropriate experience of dance and music. Percussion instruments are ideal for teaching children to listen and respond. A tambour can be used to vary the speed and dynamics of movements and create rhythms and pauses as children creep, stamp, skip, tiptoe or march around the space. An effective warm-up can be achieved using just two instruments such as a tambourine (for stepping, jumping and shaking) and a cymbal (for stretching slowly in different directions).

A good example of music as a stimulus for dance is "The Sorcerer's Apprentice" by Dukas, which is realised in Disney's well-known *Fantasia* cartoon.

The music has a narrative with clearly identifiable motifs, rhythms and melodies that relate to the characters, objects and events. A dance based on this piece of music could form a suitable unit of work for six- to eight-year-olds, lasting several sessions. Popular music such as rock 'n' roll also provides a stimulating starting point (and, of course, accompaniment) for dance; the style influences the movement qualities and structural elements of coda, verse, chorus and instrumental bridge help shape a class dance. All the units of work on the web resource have clear links to music.

Dance and Humanities

The humanities develop children's curiosity about people and the world, past and present. Geography; history; personal, social and health education; and citizenship and religious education share very close links, and in partnership they provide many curriculum topics and themes that dance can enhance and enrich.

Geography

Dance reinforces understanding of location by increasing children's understanding of the human world, environments, societies and cultures, whether it's a dance such as Builders at Work or a South African gumboot dance. Traditional stories from other cultures such as The Calabash Children and Tiddalik take the children on journeys to contrasting locations. Knowledge

Dance reinforces understanding of location.

of patterns and processes can be interpreted through dances inspired by the weather or the action of water and how these affect people and the environment. You could explore awareness of environmental change and sustainable development on a simple level by using the story *Dinosaurs and All That Rubbish* by Michael Foreman for a key stage 1 unit of work.

Map making and map reading are where dance and geography overlap. Maps provide interesting stimuli for dance (directions, routes, contours, features of the landscape and symbols); in turn, children can map their sequences and dances showing routes and using symbols. The theme of journeys, whether by magic carpet or by using Australian Aboriginal paintings, could take children to other countries and continents or contrasting climates and provide imaginative ways to combine dance and geography.

▶ *Other Units of Work With Links to Geography*

- Handa's Hen (Africa)
- Holi (India)
- Pan Gu (China)
- Our Town (other environments)
- What a Week! and Rain Again! (weather)
- Recycle! (environmental change)

Dance as a medium for exploring everyday life in the past.

History

Children can communicate their understanding of history through dance as much as they can through writing and talking. Re-creating dance of times past, from follow-the-leader chains and simple circle dances of hundreds of years ago to the energetic and athletic rock 'n' roll of the 1950s, is a perfect way of combining dance and history because history is concerned with the study of lives and lifestyles and comparing past and present. How do we know how people danced in the past? In more recent times we have costumes, paintings, photos, films, music and written descriptions to help us, but more detective work is required for discovering dances from ancient civilisations. Carvings, mosaics, sculptures and artefacts such as pots and vases, used with a bit of artistic licence, can provide interesting starting points for dance. The design of a Roman mosaic floor could suggest pathways and formations for a partner or group dance, for instance.

Dance enhances children's understanding of the ideas, beliefs, attitudes and experiences of people in the past and also helps them appreciate the social and cultural diversity of Britain and the wider world. As well as the dances themselves, dance can be a medium for exploring how people went about their everyday lives by creating settlements, working, playing and waging war. By reconstructing historical events in dance, children can empathise with characters and explore issues such as slavery and the plague. Dance can also interpret aspects of leisure and entertainment such as music, art, poetry, games and holidays and people's beliefs, such as in myths and legends. If studying the Victorians, for instance, children can explore through dance the building of the railways and canals, trips to the seaside, the contrast between rich and poor, upstairs and downstairs or child labour in factories.

Significant events can also provide topics for dance: Sea-faring explorers might stimulate a dance about sailors on board a ship, and the story of the first Olympics could provide several dance ideas.

Units of Work With Links to History

- All Join In, The Snowball (traditional dances)
- Rock 'n' Roll (dances from other times)
- Toys (toys of yesteryear)

Personal, Social and Health Education and Citizenship

Personal, social and health education (PSHE) and citizenship focus on the ability to lead confident, independent and healthy lives and to become active, informed and responsible citizens who understand and respect people's similarities and differences. In many schools PSHE is delivered through the **SEAL** strategy, which has five aspects (self-awareness, managing feelings, motivation, empathy and social skills) and six themes (new beginnings, getting on and falling out, going for goals, good to be me, relationships and changes). These themes are revisited yearly and provide plenty of opportunities for cross-curricular learning.

Dance is an ideal medium for exploring themes and issues such as friendship, bullying, racism and other moral and social issues and dilemmas. Dance can provide a secure context for exploring issues and encouraging empathy by using poems and stories such as The Loner. Dance also plays a significant role in developing children's awareness of culture and identity by experiencing dances from diverse cultures. Through dance, children learn about their bodies and how to access a healthy lifestyle. Through performance, they develop self-awareness, self-esteem and confidence, and they are able to recognise their strengths and set personal targets for development.

Dance and PSHE share many generic learning skills. Dance requires good social skills. Children learn to work together and to give and take; dance also requires good behaviour and self-discipline. High-quality performance and composition require motivation, persistence and resilience as well as the ability to evaluate and respond to constructive criticism.

Other Units of Work
With Links to PSHE and Citizenship

- Pan Gu (feelings, new beginnings)
- Holi, The Calabash Children, Tiddalik, Handa's Hen, Pan Gu (cultural diversity)
- Mission: Impossible and A Winning Dance (attaining goals, cooperation)

Religious Education

Religious education focuses on learning about and learning from religion and beliefs. Learning *about* religion involves looking at different ways of life and practices such as worship, celebration, rituals and festivals and the ways in which people express their values and beliefs, such as through art, poetry, music, dance and story. Learning *from* religion is concerned with identity, belonging and relationships—the challenges of life and the moral issues that face us. Dance is a lively and imaginative medium for exploring aspects of Christianity, Hinduism, Islam and Judaism (which form the breadth of study for key stages 1 and 2) and other religious traditions. It provides opportunities for expressing a sense of wonder and mystery and encourages children to show sensitivity and empathise with others and value diversity. In Western cultures, dance does not share a particularly close relationship with religion, unlike other traditions such as the temple dances of India and Indonesia. A perfect example of partnership between dance and religion can be seen in Alvin Ailey's *Revelations* choreographed in 1960 and based on traditional African-American spiritual songs that provide the accompaniment. The wonder and awe expressed in the opening dance to the song "I've Been Buked" are spine tingling.

Bible stories, such as the parables, creation stories, epic adventures from various religious traditions and stories that celebrate the triumph of good over evil, provide exciting contexts for dance. Special events such as harvest could be compared and contrasted through learning a Morris dance and a Bhangra dance. Other special events, such as the Hindu festivals of Holi and Diwali, can be celebrated in dance and religious symbols, such as candlelight, provide starting points for dance. Journeys such as that of the magi and the pilgrimage to the River Ganges can be interpreted through dance. The journey of the Ganges itself, together with the legend of its creation, provides an excellent stimulus for dance.

Units of Work
With Links to Religious Education

- Holi (Hindu festival)
- Pan Gu (Chinese creation story)

Dance and Information Technology

Dance encourages creative use of information technology (IT), and there are several effective ways in which dance and IT work together to enhance learning. Children can use IT to research ideas and collect information about dance, such as by looking at video clips and finding out about specific dance styles. DVDs of films that feature dances and of professional dance companies also provide effective teaching and learning tools. Information technology can be used in recording dances by devising simple notations, such as symbols for actions and floor plans showing directions. Children could draw body and group shapes using pin figures to enhance dance descriptions or instructions, and older children could demonstrate the compositional process using a PowerPoint presentation. Digital cameras, iPads and flip videos are effective self-evaluation and peer evaluation tools; they are also invaluable in capturing and celebrating dance achievements. In A Winning Dance, which uses a DVD as a starting point, the children could compose their group dances as if for a pop video, thinking about camera shots and techniques as they make video recordings of their finished products. Children can also capture and edit sound and compose and edit music to create exciting accompaniment for their dances.

Children are knowledgeable about computer and console games from an early age; these can provide imaginary dance contexts featuring chases, missions, aliens and transformations. Cyber-speak itself can be used as a stimulus for dance in key stage 2. For instance, commands such as eject, zoom, rotate, attach, pause, cut and paste could inspire movement vocabulary and develop composition skills. New technologies such as mobile phones could also stimulate a quirky dance for older children based on individual number sequences (from a list of actions numbered 0 to 9); coordinating gestures with travelling as if talking on the phone; interpreting text messages into movement; and using text message commands such as send, delete, edit as compositional devices.

Dance, Design and Technology

Design and technology are about making use of a range of materials including food, textiles and electrical and mechanical products. The processes of developing ideas, planning, making and evaluating processes and products are similar to those of developing dance ideas and planning and evaluating dances. But in design and technology, the outcome fulfills a function. The relationship between dance and design and technology can be meaningful and exciting when children design and create masks and props for dance and when they design and create model stage sets (with moving parts) for dances they have composed. They could also design and make costumes, accessories and percussion instruments to accompany their dances. Following their experience of dances about toys, younger children could make string puppets or robots out of recycled objects. A dance idea that explores the mechanical movements of levers, wheels, gears and pulleys will consolidate vocabulary and understanding of how mechanisms work.

Units of Work That Link to Design and Technology

- Toys (puppets and robots)
- Recycle (percussion instruments)

Figure 8.2 is based on a dance-initiated project about recycling for years 3 and 4 and shows the ways in which the project links together several curriculum areas. The Recycle unit is on the web resource.

Using technology in the dance lesson.

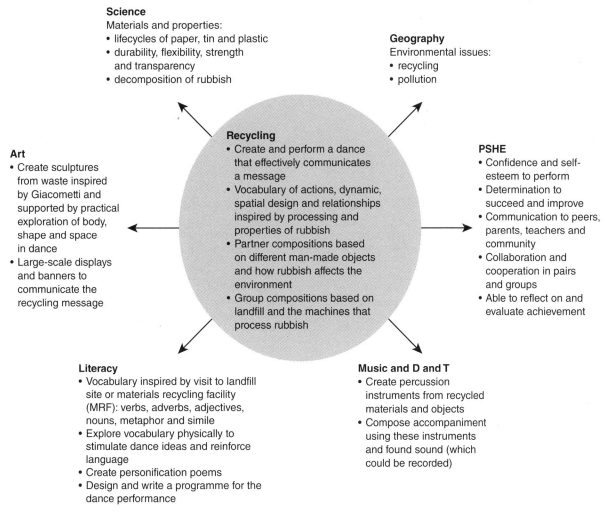

Science
Materials and properties:
• lifecycles of paper, tin and plastic
• durability, flexibility, strength and transparency
• decomposition of rubbish

Geography
Environmental issues:
• recycling
• pollution

Art
• Create sculptures from waste inspired by Giacometti and supported by practical exploration of body, shape and space in dance
• Large-scale displays and banners to communicate the recycling message

Recycling
• Create and perform a dance that effectively communicates a message
• Vocabulary of actions, dynamic, spatial design and relationships inspired by processing and properties of rubbish
• Partner compositions based on different man-made objects and how rubbish affects the environment
• Group compositions based on landfill and the machines that process rubbish

PSHE
• Confidence and self-esteem to perform
• Determination to succeed and improve
• Communication to peers, parents, teachers and community
• Collaboration and cooperation in pairs and groups
• Able to reflect on and evaluate achievement

Literacy
• Vocabulary inspired by visit to landfill site or materials recycling facility (MRF): verbs, adverbs, adjectives, nouns, metaphor and simile
• Explore vocabulary physically to stimulate dance ideas and reinforce language
• Create personification poems
• Design and write a programme for the dance performance

Music and D and T
• Create percussion instruments from recycled materials and objects
• Compose accompaniment using these instruments and found sound (which could be recorded)

Figure 8.2 Cross-curricular links in a year 3 and 4 recycling project.

Summary

This chapter has looked in detail at the way in which dance relates to and enhances each curriculum area. There is no doubt that dance can enhance and enrich learning across the curriculum and that it will contribute to a strengthened and streamlined curriculum, particularly when meaningful and imaginative links are explored. Dance provides a unique opportunity for children to explore concepts and ideas physically and to bring learning to life.

Resources for Dance

This chapter focuses on resources that support teaching and learning in dance, in addition to those that are used for stimuli. It also looks at music as accompaniment, providing information about types and styles of music, elements of music, traditional folk music and how to create and select accompaniment. The chapter also advises on the use of professional dance on film and live performances of professional dance artists to enhance the children's dance experience.

Dance requires minimal equipment and resources. The bare essentials are a reasonably sized clean space, an enthusiastic teacher and, of course, some children. "Must-have" equipment includes a sound system on which to play recorded music, a range of accompaniment and a whiteboard or flip chart for exploring and sharing key words and ideas. "Might-have" equipment, which is required occasionally, includes access to a DVD player or data projector for viewing dance, selected dance DVDs and access to a video camera or flip cameras for recording dance. Stimuli for dance (see chapter 4) can mostly be gathered from the resources that are available in the classroom and throughout the school, so this chapter focuses on dance-specific resources that support and enhance teaching and learning more generally.

A collection of suitable resources to support dance could be collected in the school over time to be shared with colleagues and with different age groups. The following resources would be suitable for the school to share or for you to keep as a kit:

- A large dice or "move it" cube for attaching actions, shapes, words, phrases or compositional ideas to decide and order movement material by chance
- A set of flash cards with action words for children to select from and explore (cards could also contain words relating to space, dynamics and relationships)
- Laminated posters of words relating to action, space, dynamics and relationships and of key words or prompts for performance, composition and appreciation (see web resource)
- A tambour and beater, tambourine and cymbal
- Wire coat hangers and clothes pegs for displaying key words, vocabulary and prompts

Other resources that stimulate and enhance movement include props such as these:

- Paper streamers (cut from rolls of crepe paper and stapled together) or gymnastics ribbons for water, fire, carnival, and so on
- Lengths of lightweight fabric to enhance movement or create environments
- Masks (white, plastic, available in sets from fancy dress suppliers) that can be sprayed or decorated for robots, mythical creatures, and so on
- Lengths of elastic (for webs or mazes)

Streamers stimulate and enhance movement.

- Laminated prints of paintings (such as those reproduced in calendars or on postcards)
- Recipe cards (free from many supermarkets) to provide movement words and images
- Poems and stories suitable for dance
- Laminated photos of dancers in interesting positions, shapes and relationships
- A collection of natural objects with interesting textures and shapes such as seashells and feathers

Children could bring in accessories for particular dance ideas, such as wellies for gumboot dancing and baseball caps for street dance.

Music for Dance

This section focuses on music as accompaniment for dance. Understanding of different types of accompaniment, how to select it and how to use it will give you confidence and will ultimately enrich the children's experience of dance. Experiencing music through dance and experiencing dance through music will result in better dancers, musicians and audiences. Musicality, or the ability to pick out the unique qualities of music and use them sensitively in performance and composition, will be enhanced by a rich range of dance and music experiences. Music is not an absolute necessity for the dance lesson, and there are times when it is more appropriate for children to explore and improvise without any accompaniment. However, music can offer these benefits:

- Background sound for creative exploration
- Mood or atmosphere
- Structure
- Meaning through narrative or lyrics
- A sense of place or time
- Style

Types of accompaniment include the following:

- Spoken word (live or recorded)
- Sounds made by dancers
- Silence
- Music and song
- Natural sounds (e.g., recorded sounds from nature)
- Found sound (e.g., recorded clocks ticking and bells ringing)

Even with silence, there will be audible aspects of dance such as the noise made by dancers breathing and their bodies in contact with the floor.

There are many styles of music, such as folk, pop, rock, country, jazz, classical, electronic, percussion and traditional. Choice of style of accompaniment and the relationship between the accompaniment and the dance largely depends on the stimulus and intention of the dance. A close relationship is where the movements match the music or interpret the lyrics, or where the musical structure provides a framework for the dance. Music sometimes provides a narrative by providing mood, setting and motifs that represent characters; an example is Prokofiev's *Peter and the Wolf*. A distant relationship is where the music provides background sound but movements are formed and structured independently of it. In the dance and music of Africa and Asia, call and response is often used—this is where the musician sets the rhythm and the dancers respond as if they are conversing.

Percussion

It is good to have access to a range of instruments, such as those normally stored on the school's music trolley, from time to time. Many dance teachers rely on having a tambour and beater, tambourine and cymbal in every dance lesson because these instruments can be used for warming up, exploring movement material, adding cues or signals to recorded music and

Gloves are easy and effective accessories to source.

aiding control. It is much easier, for instance, to control and vary the speed and dynamics of children travelling around the room with a tambour than with recorded music.

Elements of Music

The elements of music that have the closest relationship to dance are pulse, rhythm, melody, dynamics, texture and silence. These elements, together with structure, will influence the movements that dancers use.

Using a tambourine to control movement.

- **Pulse** (or beat) is the regular meter of the music.

- **Rhythm** refers to the way in which beats are grouped and may be regular (as in most pop and folk music) or irregular (which is more challenging and unpredictable). Rhythm can also be natural, such as the body rhythms of breathing and heartbeats. Most Western music tends to group beats in 2s (a march), 3s (waltz time) and 4s; the accent (emphasis) is nearly always on beat 1. The recommended accompaniment for What a Week! (in the web resource) provides various types of music and a range of rhythms for children to dance to. Occasionally you will find a piece of music in 5/4 meter, which can be dramatic, like "Mars" from *The Planets Suite* by Gustav Holst, or playful, like "Take Five" by Dave Brubeck. Words, especially in poetry, have a rhythm. Take a look at "Snow" by Walter de la Mare (1939) to see how words and movements could work rhythmically.

- **Melody** has phrasing and shape and helps to create mood. Melody might be dramatic and punchy or smoothly rising and falling.

- **Dynamics** in music refers to the volume, and this, together with **pitch** (low to high) and melody, contribute to expression.

- **Texture** is the way in which different sounds and elements are layered and is also achieved through instrumentation (different instruments playing different parts at the same time).

- **Silence** is as important to music as stillness is to dance. It can provide contrast, tension, dramatic highlights and moments of rest.

- **Structure** is the way in which the material is organised to create the whole and includes motifs, sequences, repetition and pattern. Following are the most commonly used forms (see chapter 4):
  - **Binary** is two parts: AB.
  - **Ternary** is three parts: ABA.
  - **Canon** is a round of overlapping parts.
  - **Rondo** is verse and chorus: ABCBDB.

An example of how musical structure can provide a framework for a key stage 2 dance is in table 9.1.

Traditional English Folk Music

Traditional English folk music is functional in that certain tunes are suited to particular dances, and each piece contains either 32- or 48-bar repeats. Most notated dances suggest the rhythm and the number of bars required. These are the most commonly used folk rhythms:

- Reel: 4/4 meter (e.g., "Polly Put the Kettle On")
- Jig: 6/8 meter (e.g., "Humpty Dumpty")

Task

Ask the children to listen to a piece of rock 'n' roll music other than "Blue Suede Shoes" to identify how many verses, how many choruses, how many beats for each verse or chorus, the order, what happens in the middle and how the music starts and finishes. Discuss how this information might help to structure the dance.

Table 9.1   "Blue Suede Shoes" by Carl Perkins

Structure of music	Structure of dance
Intro (A)	Three rock 'n' roll partner snapshot positions
Chorus (B)	Class unison sequence of steps (forward, backward, sideways and around) facing front
Verse (C)	Partner sequence of own steps and directions
Chorus (B)	Repeat class chorus facing partners
Instrumental (D)	Hand jive (class unison)
Verse (C)	Group sequence focusing on feet (blue suede shoes!)
Chorus (B)	Class chorus in groups
Instrumental (D)	Group hand jive
Coda (A)	Snapshot partner shapes
Chorus (B)	Class chorus (all facing front)

- Polka: 4/4 meter with an upbeat on count 1 (e.g., "Bobby Shaftoe")
- Hornpipe: 4/4 meter but slowish and with a step–hop feel
- Waltz: 3/4 meter

The phrasing of traditional folk music is normally in sections of 8 bars, the melodies of which are repeated at certain points. So a 32-bar reel might sound like this:

- A1: first 8-bar phrase
- A2: the same, repeated
- B1: second 8-bar phrase (different melody)
- B2: the same, repeated

Dancers' counts tend to be slightly different in that 16 dance counts (i.e., 16 counts for 16 steps in a folk dance) will take 8 bars of music. It does not matter which counting method you use as long as you are consistent, and actually it is far better for the children to listen and dance to the musical phrasing than try to count the beats.

Creating Accompaniment

Creating music and dance at the same time can be very exciting. An example for the early years is a narrative dance, such as Handa's Hen, which contrasts the movements of different animals. The children could suggest a suitable percussion instrument for each animal, and half the class could accompany the half that is dancing. Older children will enjoy editing their own accompaniment. For instance, A Winning Dance requires several different sections and sound effects.

Selecting Music for Dance

Dance requires a range of accompaniment, and children are receptive to various types and styles of music. If you enjoy the music, the children usually will. Effective accompaniment will most likely have dynamic variation, contrast and some sort of form and structure (repetition, pattern and sequence). You could explore your own collections and what is available in school for music lessons and assemblies, listening especially for music from diverse cultures. Compilations of music used for films, commercials and global music are particularly useful. The dance or music coordinator in school could keep a log of suitable tracks for different dance ideas and themes to share with colleagues.

The music required for a typical dance lesson would include the following:

- Lively warm-up music
- Music for exploration of the dance idea
- Calm music for cooling down

Following are suitable music sources:

- Freeplay Music at www.freeplaymusic.com. Music can be downloaded free for educational use, using the school computer.
- Audacity and Sound Forge are software programmes for editing music and creating sound tracks.
- Chris Benstead's site at www.musicfordance.net has varied and lively music that is especially good for the early years.
- Brian Madigan's site at www.brianmadigan.com has music suitable for the primary phase.

- The Sound Moves Music Company at www. andrewkristy.moonfruit.com has music suitable for the primary phase.
- *Let's Go Zudie-o* (2001) and *Let's Go Shoo-lie-Shoo* (2003), by Helen MacGregor and Bobbie Gargrave. These music resources support dance and music in the early and primary years.

Professional Dance

Study of a work, even a small part of it, enhances, reinforces, consolidates, extends and inspires the students' own work.

Jacqueline Smith-Autard (1994).

The experience of watching a live dance performance should be an entitlement for every child and bears little comparison to viewing dance on film. However, there are advantages to using dance on film as a teaching and learning resource: Viewing can be part of the dance lesson and integrated with practical tasks, and an extract can be selected and viewed several times. Children are informed and stimulated by the works of well-known artists, composers, authors, poets and playwrights from various times and places during their school life, but access to professional dance works and those from diverse cultures has not been so easy. It is now possible to access the world of dance beyond school on DVDs and the Internet. Dance on film, from well-known companies and choreographers, informs children of the professional world of dance where people choose careers in performance, choreography or dance production (costume and stage design, for instance). Dance on film also provides male role models and introduces children to dances from diverse cultures and communities.

Viewing dance on film will enhance children's knowledge of performance, composition and appreciation. It also provides valuable aesthetic experience because dance has qualities associated with meaning and feeling and involves the viewer in responding, perceiving and interpreting. The aesthetic qualities that are most appropriate to discuss in relation to primary children are sensory, formal and expressive. Sensory qualities arise from the manner in which movements are performed. Descriptive words such as *bouncy, energetic, shimmering, smooth* or *jagged* capture the feel of the movements and will enrich children's use of verbal and non-verbal language. Formal qualities relate to aspects of choreography such as design, compositional devices, form and structure, and how well they succeed in communicating the idea. Expressive qualities are the qualities through which meaning, ideas and feelings are communicated and perceived. They are often a combination of formal and sensory qualities that make the dance or dancers appear frightening, gentle, powerful or joyous.

Professional dance works feature prominently in national exams in dance and other dance courses for secondary students, where they are prescribed for study through performance, composition and appreciation. Following are some of the dance styles and origins now available on DVD and the Internet:

- Here are contemporary dance and classical ballet works by well-known choreographers and companies:
  - *Nutcracker!:* Matthew Bourne, Warner International (orphanage scene, ice-skating scene, gobstopper dance).
  - *Stamping Ground*: Jiri Kylian/Nederlands Dans Theater, Arthaus Musik (inspired by tribal dances of Australians).
  - *The Tales of Beatrix Potter*: Frederick Ashton, Opus Arte (classical ballet based on the well-known animal characters).

Viewing dance on film will inspire and enhance performance and composition.

- *Still Life at the Penguin Café*: David Bintley, Arthaus Musik (endangered species include penguins and zebra).
- *Swan Lake*: Matthew Bourne, Warner International (cygnets dance).
- *A Simple Man*: Gillian Lynne, BBC/Opus Arte (industrial scene).
- *Hobson's Choice*: David Bintley, Opus Arte.
- *Stomp Out Loud!:* Warner Vision (percussive dance using props).

- Here are films (usually musicals) that include dance:
  - *Slumdog Millionaire:* Fox Searchlight (Bollywood credits scene).
  - *Street Dance*: Vertigo Films.
  - *Hellzapoppin':* Second Sight/Universal Studios (Lindy hop section).
  - *Singin' in the Rain*: MGM Musicals/ Warner.
  - *High School Musical* series: Disney.

- Video clips on the Internet: BBC Learning Zone (www.bbc.co.uk/learningzone/clips/ dance) contains several excellent video clips of children and adults dancing in a range of styles and types, such as Bhangra, Bollywood, street dance and Tudor dance. Choreographers feature include David Bintley, Shobana Jeyasingh, Wayne McGregor, Doug Elkins, Siobhan Davies and Matthew Bourne. Some of the clips feature short but complete dances such as Jeremy Fisher from *The Tales of Beatrix Potter*.

- There are DVDs created for use in schools, together with resource packs, such as those by Ludus Dance Company (www.ludusdance. org) who have created dances and toured to schools for 25 years. Teaching packs that include DVDs of the dances and resource packs are available for schools to purchase. They are suitable for children in key stage 2 and upwards and often explore topical issues and themes that link dance with citizenship and PSHE, such as *Sold* (about child labour) and *ID:me* (about identity). Also, *A Practical Guide to Teaching Dance* (Pocknell and Smith 2007) is a book and DVD for use with key stage 3 pupils. The nine engaging units of work for 11- to 14-year-olds provide excellent progressions from key Stage 2.

- Dance programmes produced by BBC Schools Radio (www.bbc.co.uk/school-radio/subjects/dance) provide suitable resources for dance and have been widely used in primary schools since the 1950s.

They now comprise pre-recorded CDs or MP3 downloads of dance lessons with comprehensive online teachers' notes for various age groups. The content is written by dance specialists, and skills are developed progressively. The dances are based on curriculum topics and themes, and each develops over two to four sessions. Note that these programmes are intended as resources and not teacher replacements. To be effective and achieve high-quality outcomes, you must take control of the teaching and learning and make good use of the teachers' notes.

Figure 9.1 demonstrates how we respond when viewing dance on film and the features of performance, composition and appreciation that could provide areas to focus on.

To use dance on film as an effective resource:

- Be clear about the intention. Will it inform performance, composition or appreciation?
- Select a suitable extract. Keep it short and show it more than once if necessary.
- Explain the context—how the extract relates to the whole, who choreographed it, and so on.
- Consider when best to show it—in the classroom before the dance lesson begins, during the lesson or at the end. This largely depends on the purpose and intention.
- Prepare questions to guide thinking and understanding.
- Provide opportunities for paired or group discussion. Each pair or group could provide feedback on a unique aspect.
- Remember that viewing dance will enrich dance skills and vocabulary.

An example of how a viewing task can inform practical tasks for key stage 2 (A Winning Dance) is in chapter 2. Figure 9.2 provides an example for key stage 1, showing how viewing dance consolidates understanding of the dance ingredients. View the penguin (Great Auk) trio at the start of *Still Life at the Penguin Café*, choreographed by David Bintley. This analysis could be used in planning a dance experience for children in foundation stage or key stage 1.

Suitable Practical Tasks

- Explore stepping with feet turned out and upright posture with arms by sides and flexed hands.
- Explore hops, jumps and skips while keeping this posture.

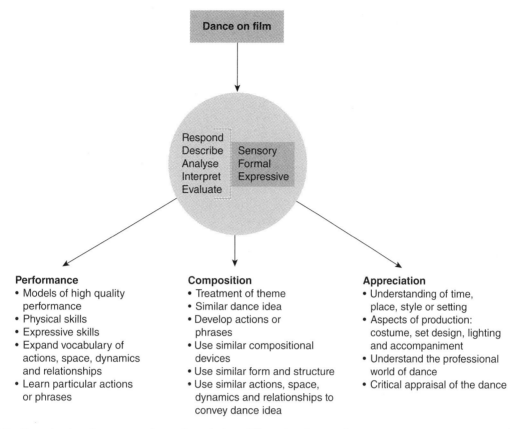

Dance on film

Respond
Describe
Analyse
Interpret
Evaluate

Sensory
Formal
Expressive

Performance
- Models of high quality performance
- Physical skills
- Expressive skills
- Expand vocabulary of actions, space, dynamics and relationships
- Learn particular actions or phrases

Composition
- Treatment of theme
- Similar dance idea
- Develop actions or phrases
- Use similar compositional devices
- Use similar form and structure
- Use similar actions, space, dynamics and relationships to convey dance idea

Appreciation
- Understanding of time, place, style or setting
- Aspects of production: costume, set design, lighting and accompaniment
- Understand the professional world of dance
- Critical appraisal of the dance

Figure 9.1 How viewing dance can enhance knowledge, skills and understanding.

- Follow the leader in twos or threes to explore travelling and pathways.
- Choose the steps that they like using best and practice in twos or threes.
- Plan the floor pattern.
- Add weaving around other dancers and stillness.

Professional Dance Artists

Professional dance artists are an invaluable resource. They bring expertise as performers or choreographers, fresh ideas, specialised knowledge of specific dance styles and high expectations of what children can achieve. They provide good role models who represent the professional world of dance. They can inspire and motivate the school community, enrich the children's dance experience, provide professional development for staff and provide a focus for cross-curricular working. Dance artists might represent small- or large-scale dance companies, or they might work as individuals in the local community. Inputs could range from one-off workshops to week-long intensive residencies or longer-term partnerships. Residencies could involve children from a number of schools, including partner secondary schools. Successful residencies often involve opportunities to watch a live performance, training for teachers, workshops with children to stimulate and develop dance ideas, and a final sharing or performance. An example of a successful partnership project is on the DVD *Primary Dance: Using Dance to Support Learning Across the Curriculum* (AfPE et al. 2011), which demonstrates the high-quality outcomes that can be achieved when a school is committed to dance and to working with professional artists.

Productive relationships between schools and dance artists require the following:

- Good communication and collaborative planning
- Clear objectives and outcomes
- Appropriate match of dance artists and workshop content to children's needs
- Clearly understood expectations by school, staff, artists and children
- A realistic budget
- An agreed method of project evaluation by all involved

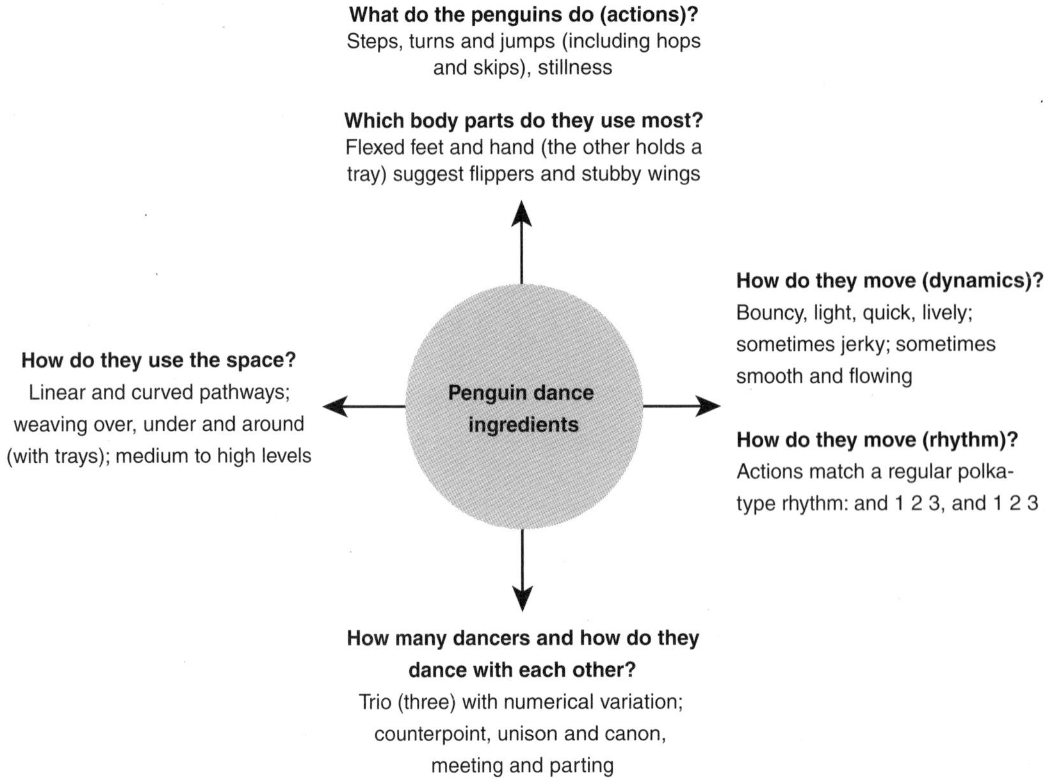

What do the penguins do (actions)?
Steps, turns and jumps (including hops and skips), stillness

Which body parts do they use most?
Flexed feet and hand (the other holds a tray) suggest flippers and stubby wings

How do they move (dynamics)?
Bouncy, light, quick, lively; sometimes jerky; sometimes smooth and flowing

How do they move (rhythm)?
Actions match a regular polka-type rhythm: and 1 2 3, and 1 2 3

Penguin dance ingredients

How do they use the space?
Linear and curved pathways; weaving over, under and around (with trays); medium to high levels

How many dancers and how do they dance with each other?
Trio (three) with numerical variation; counterpoint, unison and canon, meeting and parting

Figure 9.2 Analysis of the great auk dance in *Still Life at the Penguin Café*.

To work in a school as a dance artist, you will need to know the following:

- What resources and equipment are available
- The dance space
- School procedures and policies (e.g., changing, behaviour, lesson times, break times and lunch times)
- The children's prior experience, achievement and needs
- How the experience will contribute to learning in dance and the curriculum

The school should do the following:

- Be satisfied that the dance artist complies with safe-guarding procedures.
- Be assured that the dance artist has appropriate training and insurance.
- Remember that this is a unique professional development opportunity for staff.
- Ensure that a teacher is present at all times and responsible for behaviour and health and safety.

- Consider how to follow up the visit or develop the work initiated by the dance artist.

To find out more about dance artists and how to access them, schools can contact these organisations:

- Local dance venues, who often promote workshops and residencies in connection with visiting dance companies
- Local and regional dance and performing arts agencies

Primary schools could also contact local secondary schools and colleges, who may have school-based dance companies or performance groups.

Summary

We are blessed with a wide range of resources for dance. In recent years, technology has made these even more accessible. As far as music is concerned, we are now spoilt for choice. It is therefore important that you carefully select resources, whether physical or human, so that they inspire, stimulate and enhance learning.

Glossary

abstract dance—Non-representational but having features that denote the essence of the original.

accent—Placement of stress on a beat or action.

accessory—Additional item of costume that is worn by a dancer.

accompaniment—The sound that goes with a dance.

accumulation—When a dancer begins a series of phrases and others join in until all perform in unison.

action and reaction—When a dancer moves and another responds with a movement; a conversation in movement.

aesthetic—Judged to be tasteful or beautiful.

alignment—Correct placement of body parts in relation to each other.

auditory (as in stimulus)—Heard.

Bhangra—Energetic and acrobatic folk dance originating from farming communities in the Punjab; it now forms the basis of social dances in Punjabi communities.

Bharatanatyam—Classical Indian dance style characterised by fast footwork and intricate hand gestures.

binary—A composition in two parts.

Bollywood—South Asian dance style associated with film industry, combining elements of classical, folk and street dance.

canon—When the same movements overlap in time.

chance—Choreographic approach that uses random methods to determine or manipulate material such as throwing dice or a die.

choreographic approaches—How choreographers create and use movement material.

choreographic devices—Methods used in developing, varying and repeating movement material.

climax—The most significant part of a composition.

collage—Choreographic approach that pieces together a number of dance ideas under a unifying theme.

comic dance—Type of dance outcome that expresses humour.

complementary—Actions or shapes that are similar but not exactly the same.

contact—The use of touch, body parts in contact, sharing weight and taking weight.

contemporary—A group of dance styles outside of classical ballet that originated early in the 20th century and was created in response to the conditions of contemporary life.

continuity—Flow of a movement.

contraction—Shortening of muscles, part or whole of the body.

coordination—Combining two body parts or actions.

core stability—Use of the deep muscles in the abdominal and pelvic region to stabilise the body during movement.

counterbalance—When two or more dancers use each other to achieve a balanced position.

counterpoint—When two or more dancers perform different phrases simultaneously.

countertension—When two or more dancers use their own and each other's strength to achieve support, as in pulling.

dance drama—Combines elements of dance and drama in a narrative form.

differentiation—Enabling individuals and groups of children to achieve.

dramatic dance—A type of dance that might be narrative, where a story unfolds, or it could explore an aspect of the human conditions, such as an issue, mood or emotion, in a non-narrative way.

dynamics—Movement qualities that provide the colour and texture of movement. The elements commonly referred to today are force, speed and continuity (or flow). In music, refers to the volume; this, together with pitch (low to high) and melody, contribute to expression.

dynamic stretch—Moving muscles and joints in a slow and controlled manner as part of continuous movement.

effort actions—Actions (including floating, gliding and pressing) that result in combining the elements of weight, space, time and flow.

elevation—Being airborne, such as jumping.

expressive skills—Aspects that contribute to performance energy and artistry and engage the audience, such as focus and musicality.

extension—Lengthening the muscles or limbs.

flexibility—Relating to the range of movement in joints and muscles.

focus—Where the dancer looks; using the eyes to enhance performance.

form—Overall shape and structure.

formations—Shapes and patterns created in space by dancers.

formative assessment—Assessment for learning; ongoing and continuous assessment during the learning process.

fundamental movement skills—The movements that create a foundation for more complex skills or movement patterns; categorised as body management, locomotor and object control skills.

general space—The dance space.

genre—A family of dance styles such as contemporary, ballet, jazz, ballroom, urban and folk. Each genre has a range of styles that share similar features.

gesture—The movement of part of the body or the whole body that does not involve weight bearing or transfer of weight.

highlights—Important moments in the dance.

isolation—Moving a body part independently of other body parts.

jumping (or elevation)—When the body leaves and returns to the floor using the feet and legs as springs.

Kathak—A classical style of dance that originated in North India; features include complex footwork, fast spins and sudden poses.

Kathakali—A narrative dance style from Southwest India that is traditionally danced by men. It is characterised by dramatic and vigorous actions and stylised mime, makeup and costume.

kinaesthetic—Referring to the awareness of movement and position of parts of the body by means of sensory organs in the muscles and joints.

learning outcome—What the learner knows, understands or is able to do that is new.

level—In relation to the ground (i.e., low, medium or high).

lyrical—A type of dance that interprets music and that has a light, melodic quality.

melody—The arrangement of notes to make a tune.

mimetic—Literal or representational actions.

mirror—Reflecting an action or shape.

mobility—Range of motion in a joint or the ability to move fluently from action to action.

Modern Educational Dance—Term describing dance in education, commonly used between the 1940s and 1970s.

motif—Movement phrase that captures the essence of the dance and that can be repeated and developed.

multiple intelligences—Different types of intelligence (visual-spatial, linguistic, kinaesthetic, logical-mathematical, musical, interpersonal, intrapersonal, naturalistic) categorised by Howard Gardner.

musicality—The ability to use the unique qualities of the accompaniment in performance.

narrative—Dance that tells a story.

Natya—Element of mime in Asian dance.

Nritta—Stylised poses and footwork patterns in Asian dance.

Nritya—Elements of mime and movement in Asian dance.

numerical variation—How the number of dancers in a group is used.

peer assessment—Evaluating and giving feedback to others.

personal space—Space around the body.

phrase—Sequence of actions.

physical literacy—Ability to instruct the body to perform an action accurately and confidently and to recognise the physical, social, cognitive and emotional attributes required to do so effectively.

posture—Relative position of body parts.

projection—Giving out appropriate performance energy to communicate with the audience.

props—Portable objects that are used in dance.

pulse—Regular beat of a piece of accompaniment.

pulse raising—Activities that increase the heart rate.

pure dance—A dance that is concerned with movement itself.

relationships—How dancers move with each other.

rhythm—Repeated patterns of sounds or movements.

rondo—Musical form with an alternating and repeated section, such as a chorus.

scheme of work—A long-term curriculum plan that covers a year and one or more key stages.

SEAL—Social and emotional aspects of learning; a national strategy, introduced to English schools in 2005, aimed at developing qualities and skills to promote positive behaviour and effective learning. The five aspects are self-awareness, managing feelings, motivation, empathy and social skills; the six themes are new beginnings, getting on and falling out, going for goals, good to be me, relationships and changes.

self-assessment—Encourages children to take responsibility for their own progress and promotes independent learning.

silence—Can provide contrast, tension, dramatic highlights and moments of rest.

simultaneous—Movements that happen at the same time, such as legs and arms shooting out in a star jump.

stamina—Ability to maintain movement over periods of time.

starting point—A strategy, such as list of action words, that initiates movement.

static stretch—Stretch that is held still for at least 10 seconds.

stillness—Ability to control equilibrium or to stop a movement.

stimulus (or **stimuli**)—Inspiration for movement.

strength—Muscular power.

structure—The way in which the material is organised to create the whole and comprises motifs, sequences, repetition and pattern. Binary, ternary, canon and rondo are the most common structures.

style—Characteristic way of dancing.

successive—Movements that happen one after the other (e.g., a rippling arm action).

summative assessment—Judgements about attainment made after the learning has taken place.

supple—Flexible (relating to the range of motion in joints and muscles).

technical skills—Physical aspects, such as alignment and coordination, that enable a dancer to perform effectively.

technique—A specific way of moving according to particular conventions.

ternary—Composition in three parts.

texture—The way in which sounds and elements are layered; it is also achieved through instrumentation (different instruments playing different parts at the same time).

thinking styles—Different types of thinking, such as abstract and concrete sequential, categorised by A.F. Gregorc.

traditional—A long-established custom or style.

transitions—Linking actions between phrases or sections of a dance.

travelling—Transfer of weight in order to move across space by using the feet or other body parts (e.g., stepping, sliding, crawling or slithering).

turning—Rotation around an axis.

type—Category of dance composition that has a distinctive outcome, such as narrative or comic.

unison—Everyone performing the same movement.

unit of work—A medium term curriculum plan that introduces a new topic or set of skills.

VAK—Visual, auditory and kinaesthetic learning styles.

visual—Seen.

References

Chapter 1

Dance UK. 2006. *Dance manifesto.* London: Author.

Department for Culture, Media and Sport, NDTA, QCA, YDE. 2005. *Dance links: A guide to delivering high quality dance for children and young people.* London: Author.

Chapter 2

Gough, M. 1999. *Knowing dance: A guide for creative teaching.* London: Dance Books.

HMSO. 1909. *The syllabus of physical exercises for schools.* London: Author.

HMSO. 1933. *The syllabus of physical training for schools.* London: Author.

HMSO. 1952. *Physical education in the primary school.* London: Author.

Laban, R. 1948. *Modern educational dance.* London: Macdonald & Evans.

Singin' in the rain. 1952. (Donen, S., and G. Kelley, directors). MGM Musicals.

Smith-Autard, J.M. 2002. *The art of dance in education, second edition.* London: A&C Black.

Street dance. 2010. (Giwa, M., and D. Pasquini, directors). Vertigo Films.

Chapter 3

Humphrey, D. (Barbara Pollack, Ed.). 1959. *The art of making dances.* London: Holt, Rinehart and Winston.

Chapter 4

Gardner, H. 1993. *Frames of mind: The theory of multiple intelligences.* New York: Basic Books.

Gregorc, A.F. 1986. *An adult's guide to style.* Gregorc Associates. Available: http://gregorc.com/books.html#id1.

Humphrey, D. (Barbara Pollack, Ed.). 1959. *The art of making dances.* London: Holt, Rinehart and Winston.

Lynne, G., Davies, C., and Northern Ballet Theatre. 2010. *A simple man.* London: BBC, Opus Arte DVD.

Mosston, M., and Ashworth, S. 1986. *Teaching physical education, third edition.* Columbus, OH: Merrill.

National Resource Centre for Dance. 1988. *Coming home (Dzikunu).* Surrey: University of Surrey.

Chapter 6

Gargrave, B., and Trotman, S. 2003. *TOP Dance Handbook.* Loughborough: Youth Sport Trust.

Jarvis, Y. 2005. Dance with mixed gender groups. *Dance Matters,* 42: 18.

Chapter 7

Assessment Reform Group. 2002. Assessment for learning. www.aaia.org.uk.

Lowden, M. 1989. *Dancing to learn.* Lewes, East Sussex: Falmer Press.

Youth Dance England. 2011. *Progression in dance framework for 3–19 years.* Available: www.ndta.org.uk/publications/the-dance-frame-work-complete-package/.

Chapter 8

DfES. 2003. *Excellence and enjoyment: A strategy for primary schools*: London: HMSO.

Chapter 9

AfPE, Sports Coach UK and Youth Sports Trust. 2011. *Primary dance: Using dance to support learning across the curriculum* (DVD). Available: www.youthsporttrust.org.

de la Mare, W. 1939. *Snow.* Full poem available: www.poemhunter.com/poem/snow-2/.

MacGregor, H., and Gargrave, B. 2001. *Let's go, Zudie-o: Creative activities for dance and music.* London: A&C Black.

MacGregor, H., and Gargrave, B. 2003. *Let's go, Shoolie-Shoo: Creative activities for dance and music.* London: A&C Black.

Pocknell, L., and Smith, F. 2007. *A practical guide to teaching dance.* London: Association for Physical Education and National Dance Teachers Association.

Smith-Autard, J.M. 1994. *The art of dance in education.* London: A&C Black.

Recommended Reading

Dance UK. 2002. *Dance teaching essentials*. London: Author.

Gough, M. 1999. *Knowing dance: a guide for creative teaching*. Dance Books Ltd.

Harlow, M., and Rolfe, L. 1992. *Let's dance: a handbook for teachers*. BBC Educational Publishing.

Sexton, K. 2004. *The dance teacher's survival guide*. Dance Books Ltd.

Upton, E., and Paine, L. 1996. *Up the sides and down the middle*. Devon: Southgate.

Whitlam, P. 2012. Safe practice in physical education and sport. Published on behalf of afPE by Coachwise. Leeds.

Youth Dance England. 2010. *Dance in and beyond schools*. Available: http://www.yde.org.uk/documents/Publications/Dance%20In%20and%20Beyond%20Schools_An%20essential%20guide%20to%20dance%20teaching%20and%20learning.pdf.

About the NDTA

National Dance Teachers Association (NDTA) is the only association whose sole remit is dance in education. It is a registered charity and limited company by guarantee and is a membership organisation representing dance teachers in primary and secondary schools.

The NDTA seeks to ensure that all young people in the UK have equal access to a high-quality dance education. To achieve this, the association works with teachers, schools, government departments and arts and education agencies. They actively lobby for dance in the curriculum and assist in shaping policy relating to the quality, nature, range and scope of dance in the education sector.

NDTA is successful in raising the profile of dance at a national level through their website, their termly publication dancematters, their respected professional development programme and the development and dissemination of good practice.

About the Author

Lyn Paine is an experienced teacher trainer who has taught dance to all ages and has led training for the National Dance Teachers Association and AQA awarding body. Lyn has written several dance resources and also many dance programmes for BBC Education. She has directed schools' dance performances at the Bournemouth International Centre and Royal Albert Hall. She also has worked on many other inspiring cross-arts and cross-cultural projects for children.